—Grandparents Can—

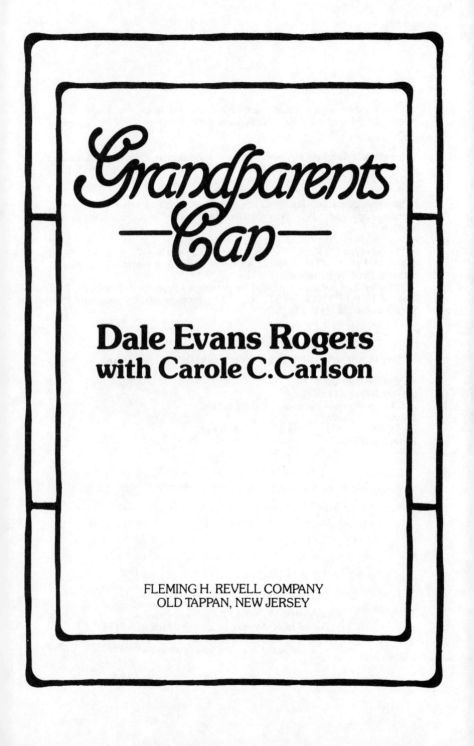

Grandparents Can

Dale Evans Rogers
with Carole C. Carlson

FLEMING H. REVELL COMPANY
OLD TAPPAN, NEW JERSEY

Library of Congress Cataloging in Publication Data

Rogers, Dale Evans.
  Grandparents can!
  1. Grandparents—Religious life. I. Carlson,
Carole C. II. Title.
BV4529.R63   1983   248.8'5   82-18622
ISBN 0-8007-1343-5

Contents

5

Introduction

Dale hears one question all over the world. Whether she is speaking in Peoria or appearing on national television, people want to know, "Why do you keep up this pace? Why don't you retire?"

Her answer is this: "The reason I keep doing what I'm doing at my age, witnessing to the power of Christ and trying to interest people in reading the Bible for the rules of life, is because I care about my grandchildren."

Dale is not a grandmother who constantly baby-sits or who frequently sees her grandchildren. Many grandmothers and grandfathers could relate more personal stories than she is able to do. However, she is using her God-given talents in the way in which the Lord directs her. If the time comes when He wants her to play another role, she will not try out for the part—she will accept it wholeheartedly.

Dale Evans Rogers is an unassuming celebrity. The jewels she wears are not for show, but are reminders of special people or occasions. She eats in coffee shops and drives her own small model car. It's only when someone thrusts a pen and paper under her nose, for an autograph, that you realize, *This lady is famous!*

The source material has come from experience and time-tested principles. The wonderful gal who has made you cry and laugh with her will provoke you to think what grandparents can (and can't) do.

Our special thanks to Georgiana Walker, who provided the thoughtful compilation of books and records for gift giving.

Most of all, we are grateful for all of you who are starring in this production: our wonderful families on earth and in heaven.

CAROLE CARLSON
Grandma, of course

1

... Change the World!

> "Over the river and through the wood, to Grand-
> mother's house we go."

What do we find at Grandma's? Fresh baked cookies and
cold milk? The Parcheesi game laid out on the table, with a
bowl of popcorn nearby? Not any more. The traditional grandmother, with her inevitable apron and hand-crocheted antima-
cassars is a fictional character. And Grandpa, walking through
the woods with his fishing pole and a grandson by his side?
That's only on a Norman Rockwell collectible.

Today Grandmother may be clerking in a department store,
working in an office, or writing a book, and be more familiar
with microwave cooking than jelly making. Grandfather is
working a nine-to-five and perfecting his golf game.

Most grandparents today fulfill untraditional roles. Some
live far away from their children and grandchildren. Many are
working and have little to do with their grandchildren, except
brag about them.

Distance is only one barrier that separates grandparents and
their grandchildren. One grandmother said, "I've raised my
kids and done my job. Now it's their turn, and I'll live my own
life. I'll see them if I'm needed or invited, but none of this free
baby-sitting service for me!"

Cracks in the family structure, due to divorce, death, or disagreements, may place the three-generation relationship in
jeopardy. Complex in-law, step-in-law, and multiple sets of
grandparents further complicate the scene.

What has happened to the present generation of grandparents? We seem to be set apart from our grandchildren. Can we establish those important bonds that provide the stability we need in our families today?

We have placed so much emphasis on *things* that we have tended to lose the importance of relationships. However, I believe it's never too late to change, and it's time we put grandparenting back on the priority list of important skills to be learned. Yes, *learned.* No one is born knowing how to be a grandparent. Suddenly we are thrust into that role, and what we do with it can be one of the most important contributions we make during the time the Lord gives us here on earth!

Grandparents can be a powerful force. In the United States, one third of the population is over forty-five years old. By 1985 the population in the grandparent age bracket will number over 71 million.

However, in all the reams that have been written on families, parenting, and marriage, grandparents are generally ignored. I'm here to shout, "Hey, we're important."

We grandparents have a lot to offer:

> Experience (good and bad)
>> Tolerance (after all, we've had more bumps)
>>> Wisdom (we've survived to the third generation)

Experience doesn't always lead to tolerance and wisdom, although it gives us a certain edge. The Bible says, "If any one supposes that he knows anything, he has not yet known as he ought to know" (I Corinthians 8:2 NAS). In other words, I don't think I have all the answers to the skills of grandparenting. However, at this writing I do have sixteen grandchildren and six great-grandchildren who have been the subjects of various grandparent experiments throughout the years.

I'll never forget when I looked at our first grandchild. It was as thrilling as opening night in Madison Square Garden.

Mindy was just three weeks old when Roy and I went to Yreka to see her. When I held that precious child, a feeling of such overwhelming love came upon me, that I thought I would burst. Here was a part of me, an extension of my seed in another human being. I felt such a bond with her, almost a sacred glow. God had trusted my son and daughter-in-law with this gift, but Roy and I had a responsibility, too.

When we were told that Mindy was born without one hip socket, I disintegrated into tears. Instead of a pillar of strength, I became a bowl of Jell-O. Perhaps I felt, for a moment, that we had such a tragedy with our own little Robin that it was unfair for the next generation to be dealt bitter blows. I remember that my mother walked over to me, took me by the shoulders, and shook me. She said, "Look, Tom and Barbara need you now. You can't lose control of yourself."

When I looked at my son and saw the stamina of faith in his face, I realized that this boy of mine received much of his strength from the Lord as a result of his grandmother, my mother. Could I do any less for his children?

Due to the faith and prayers of her parents, grandparents, and friends, and the skilled doctors at the Shrine Hospital, in San Francisco, within a year and a half, Mindy was walking. Today she is a missionary with Youth With a Mission, the wife of minister Jon Petersen, and working in the heart of Amsterdam, ministering to the needs of people in that city. When I visited her in their little apartment in the inner city and watched the way they were raising three beautiful children, I remembered my foolish tears when she was born.

We look at a child and want physical perfection. God gives us a child as a sacred trust.

Faith in God's ways is not a one-time experience. Faith wavers and fades, then grows and becomes strong. How could my faith have stumbled when I first knew of Mindy's hip handicap? My own first baby, precious little Robin, was a borderline mongoloid child. Yet, because of Robin's short two years on earth and as a result of a little book, *Angel Unaware,* which the Lord directed me to write, many parents of retarded children gained new strength and understanding.

Grandparents, we cannot spare our own children from heartache, nor can we deny them the pain of growing and the joy of searching.

As the grandchildren have arrived—and then the great-grandchildren—I have discovered that I truly love being Grandma. When our eldest daughter, Cheryl, declared, "Mom, my children are not calling you Nana, Mama Dale, or Grandma Dale, they are going to call you Grandma," I was delighted! It is a privilege and an honor to be Grandma and Grandpa without all of the sophisticated trappings and cutesy names that are flung around. On the other hand, a businessman I know loved being called Pom-pom by his granddaughter, although his outward image is very proper.

My great-grandchildren call me GiGi, which is an abbreviation for great-grandmother (a mouthful for a little kisser). I look at them and inwardly pray, "Lord, please let them be free in You; help us grandparents do what we can with the years we have left to preserve freedom for them."

Being a grandparent gives a person a new outlook on life. The most dignified executive may find himself in the unlikely role of "playing horsey," on the floor, with a squealing grandchild riding the bucking bronc. The woman who had been complaining about minor aches and lack of energy finds herself spending hours walking through an amusement park or pushing a two-year-old on the swing in the park. Life has been renewed!

I realize that not everyone who has this new role thrust upon him or her feels ecstatic over the idea. Some new grandparents feel they have reached a crossroads and they have left behind:

Youth—that elusive stage that America worships.
Parental control—the kids are now the parents!
Freedom—new demands will be placed on their time and ability.

But there is joy in being a grandparent! And people who have joy in their lives can change the world around them. The other day I looked out my window and saw a wonderful sight. For some time I had watched this particular man, bent a little from years, his eyes cast down as he walked determinedly for his daily exercise. He never smiled, and the print of the morning headlines seemed to be on his expression. Then one day he went by again, but his entire countenance had changed. He was looking ahead, beaming with joy and pride, and pushing a small child in a stroller. Whether or not that child was his grandchild, I don't know. But there was an unmistakable joy on his face, which transferred itself to everyone who saw him. The Bible says: ". . . A joy from generation to generation" (Isaiah 60:15 NAS).

Once I studied Scripture references on that word. By the time I had counted two hundred Bible verses that referred to joy, I stopped, realizing that the Scriptures are filled with joy.

The smile of a child, giving joy to another, is something that can be transferred. Can you imagine what changes could be made in the world, simply by passing on joy?

D. J. is one of my challenges and joys. He is my son Dusty's and daughter-in-law Linda's little boy and has been tagged with those executive initials, which seem strangely appropriate for him. When he was only five, he had a certain authoritative air about him that made his preposterous stories seem believable.

One Monday morning, during kindergarten share time, D. J. was trying to think of something interesting to tell about his weekend. "We got three rabbits at our house," he said proudly.

"Wonderful, D. J., what do they look like?"

"Oh, one is white all over, and another one is black all over, and another one is white with a black nose."

When he went home, D. J. told his mother the rabbit story. Linda said, firmly, "D. J. that's a lie. You don't have any rabbits. Now you go back to school and tell the truth."

The next day, D. J. said, "We only have two rabbits. Bo [the dog] killed one."

The next day when he went to school he said, "Well, Bo got the other two."

His way of getting rid of the lie was to tell two more. When I heard about it, I pulled him up on my lap and said, "You know, D. J., it's always best to tell the truth, because then you only have to tell a story once."

Whenever I catch myself exaggerating, I think of D. J. and his three rabbits. How many more stories would I need to tell to cover up?

D. J. is only one of the gifts I have. Perhaps one of the most difficult things for us grandparents to grasp is that our children and our grandchildren are gifts from God. We were instruments in forming the genes, but He gave them to us. The Psalmist says, "Behold, children are a gift of the Lord; The fruit of the womb is a reward" (Psalms 127:3).

Hear me, grandparents: Cherish the times with your grandchildren or those children you have made your adopted grandchildren. Listen, children and grandchildren: Consider the golden times you have with the precious gift God has given you, in the form of your grandparents.

Sometimes we find it hard to remember, as we reach the age where we have accumulated some of the material treasures of life, that these are transitory, but lives and memories are permanent.

We have such a privilege in being able to share in the lives of our grandchildren. It's almost like having a second chance with another generation after we've made all our mistakes with their mothers and fathers. A friend of mine told me that she is a more loving disciplinarian with her grandchildren than she had been with her children. For one thing, she's not as exhausted as she was in the days when she was younger and involved in the thousand and one tasks every young mother has spread before her.

Grandparenting is a two-way street. While we have the opportunity to change the world around us, we also have the need to be allowed to touch the lives of others. We long to know that:

We are valuable to someone.
    We can be useful to someone.
        We can retain dignity with aging.

In family-oriented cultures, where the oldest members stayed with the younger ones, sharing experiences, grandparents were not just tolerated, but loved and respected. For instance, the Japanese have a Respect for the Elderly Day, which is a national holiday. On a person's sixty-first birthday, there is a special occasion to honor elders and express affection for them.

That's really special. In the United States we have Mother's Day (to sell candy and flowers) and Father's Day (for the necktie industry); but Grandparent's Day, in September, on the first Sunday following Labor Day, is scarcely noticed.

Recently a lovely young woman said to me, "Is there something wrong with me because I can't wait to be a grandmother? I just love babies."

No, my friend, it's natural for a woman to look with joyful anticipation toward being a grandmother. This woman thought she was the oddball because so many of her friends dreaded the status of grandmother.

Our wonderful grandchildren and great-grandchildren are

such special blessings. If I were widowed, it would be difficult for me to live alone in a place where children were not allowed. Much of the sunshine would go out of my life if our children couldn't bring their children to our home.

Roy says I've always been a crusader of some sort. Well, that's not exactly true. It's only been within recent years, as we've watched the erosion of family values and personal relationships eating at the heart of America, that I've become more vocal about such things. Now I really feel like picking up the banner again for the cause of the forgotten minority.

What can grandparents do? Grandparents can change the world, that's what! Now wait a minute. You might say, "Are you trying to tell me that grandparents can make a dent in this chaotic mess we call society?" Yes, we can. And in the process we will have more challenges and more rewards than in any role we've ever had to play!

> My grandma likes to play with God,
> They have a kind of game.
> She plants the garden full of seeds,
> He sends the sun and rain.
>
> She likes to sit and talk with God
> And knows he is right there.
> She prays about the whole wide world,
> Then leaves us in his care.
>
> ANN JOHNSON
> Age 8

2

... Listen (And You Shall Hear)

What's a grandma?
"A grandma used to be a real mom, but then she gets
very old and changes into a grandma."

ANDREW
Age 5

Do you know a sure sign of age? It's when we say, "Now
when I was your age...," and you can add a hundred pious
statements, which are accompanied by solemn head shaking:

    ... I walked to school, no matter what the weather.
     ... I wasn't allowed to stay out after ten.
      ... I did my chores before I went to play.

And the child or young person listens to you, shrugs his
shoulders, and cancels further communication.

I have had to learn to listen, because I love to talk. Listening
is a trait that will make us appear smarter than we are. Also,
when we listen, we make the other person feel important.
Every day we see the results of those children who do not have
a sense of self-worth. However, when someone takes the time
to listen to them, to encourage them, their lives may be
changed.

A young girl in her early teens, living in an affluent neighborhood, took an overdose of sleeping pills one night. Her parents were busy with careers and didn't have a clue that their
daughter was severely depressed. She had been struggling in an
exclusive private school to attain the grade average that was

expected of her. Perhaps she didn't think she could live up to
the rigid expectations of her family. But what would have happened if that bright teenager had someone who had listened to
her frustrations?

It is of no small significance that suicide ranks second in
cause of death among teenagers. Why is this, in view of our in-
tellectual, supertechnological society? I believe it is due to lack
of love and willingness to take the time to really listen—to
communicate.

Although we grandparents are often accused of reminiscing
about days gone past, certainly if we took time to share our
own fears and failings, we might invite the confidences of our
grandchildren. We're not saints, and the younger generation
should know that! Only through God's grace can anyone survive and have hope today.

What do the kids really think of us? Here's a letter that was
in a West Coast newspaper:

"What a Grandmother Is"

A grandmother is a lady who has no children of her
own, so she likes other people's little girls. A grandfather
is a man grandmother. He goes for walks with the boys
and they talk about fishing and tractors and like that.

Grandmas don't have to do anything except be there.
They're old, so they shouldn't play hard or run. It is
enough if they drive us to the market where the pretend
horse is and have lots of dimes ready. Or if they take us
for walks, they should slow down past things like pretty
leaves or caterpillars. They should never ever say "Hurry
up."

Usually they are fat, but not too fat to tie kids' shoes.
They wear glasses and funny underwear. They can take
their teeth out and gums off.

It is better if they don't typewrite or play cards except with us. They don't have to be smart, only answer questions like why dogs hate cats and how come God isn't married. They don't talk baby talk like visitors do, because it is hard to understand. When they read to us they don't skip, or mind if it is the same story again.

Everybody should try to have one, especially if you don't have television, because grandmas are the only grownups who have got time.

                                        BY A NINE-YEAR-OLD GIRL

To listen to children is not too difficult, because we are usually so enchanted with what they are saying. We love to repeat the funny things, because they lighten our hearts and provide a source of amusing incidents.

During much of a child's life, he is being told what to do, when to do it, how to do it, and what not to do. He is being talked at. When you talk with him and listen to what he is saying, you will really be someone special. More important, that grandchild will feel special, too.

It seems to me that the greatest plus in a willingness to listen is that it provides one of the valuable tools a child needs to build his self-esteem. We're living in a time when society judges human worth by outward appearances and personal talent. The world has an unjust attitude of praising the beautiful and the intelligent and relegating the unattractive and mentally inferior to third-rate status.

The effects of a child's lack of personal worth are compounded. As small children suffer from inferiority, it builds in the teenage years and results in adults who are unable to cope with the pressures of living because of the years of conditioning in poor self-image they have received.

We all know the problems. We see teens in the drug culture; we watch them go into the cults in order to get the acceptance they lacked in their homes and churches; we agonize over where we have gone wrong as parents or grandparents. Problems are obvious. Suggestions for solutions are more creative.

Let's talk listening strategies. Certainly the attention we give to our grandchildren during the early years is different from the rap sessions we have with them in their teens and from the empathy we have for them as adults.

Rock Is Back

Some years ago baby departments sold bottle proppers, those stuffed little pillows with a strap to hold the bottle until the baby was old enough to grasp it with his two little fists. Mother was free to do the housework or take care of other children. When Grandma came to visit, she would take over and hold the baby, spending tireless hours rocking him to sleep.

Today, rocking is in style again. When I rocked my grandchildren, I sang songs like "Jesus Loves Me" and "Over the Rainbow." Today the grandchildren still love the rocking chairs in our house. Somehow I think every home should have one. In a high-speed society, there's something soothing about swaying back and forth.

Also, babies and small children should hear our voices, even when they don't understand words. One young mother said, when she brought her first baby home from the hospital, she just fed him, diapered him, and talked to herself. Her mother came in and said, "Honey, your baby is a real person. Talk to him."

Word of warning here, for grandmothers in particular: Babies haven't changed much over the years, but methods of caring for them have! Never criticize your daughter's or daughter-in-law's ideas on baby care or equipment. The new parents are being told by their own doctor what current methods are, and they are going to listen to him, not to you.

Grandparents may be shocked by some of the new procedures, but there will be a lot more understanding between the generations if we realize that our children are adults now, and this is their style.

Cloth diapers or paper, home delivery or hospital, breastfeeding or bottle, father in the delivery room or not, these are all issues for parents, not grandparents. One of the best ways to begin a wonderful relationship with that new grandchild is to give advice to his parents only when asked.

How to Talk With Children

By the time we are grandparents we may have learned the trick of talking with children. The first step is to stop talking so much and listen to them.

I know from personal experience what working parents are up against. Being in the entertainment business for much of our lives, Roy and I were away from home a lot—too much of the time. Our older children were deprived of much of our attention during those years when we were spending twelve to fourteen hours a day on a TV series. We had so little time to listen.

Now, as a grandma, I find myself struggling with the same challenges. However, I realize how fast the years go by and know that if we listen to our grandchildren when they are small, they may share the important issues in their lives with us when they are in the turbulent teens.

Children are emotional, not rational, and if we are going to establish any sort of rapport with them, it will be on an emotional basis. For instance, let's look at a situation that is quite common. Little Susan, age five-and-a-half, has just been told

that she can't go over to Karen's house to play. Mother has her
reasons and chooses not to go into a long explanation with
Susan.

"No, you can't go to Karen's house this afternoon. Go to
your room and play with your new doll-house furniture."

Mother is tired and right now has so many pressures in her
day that she's just wishing she could sit down with the latest
magazine and a cup of coffee. *Only for a minute, Lord, just let
me have some peace!*

Grandma sizes up the situation as she walks by Susan's door
and sees her little granddaughter cramming her bathing suit, a
nightgown, a sweater, and a stuffed rabbit into her Snoopy
totebag.

"Going somewhere?"

"I'm going to run away."

"Do you need some food to take along?"

"Nope, I'm going to a restaurant."

"You're going to a restaurant. Then you must have a lot of
money for that."

Susan ignores that remark of Grandma's. Money is not the
issue, it's not getting her own way. Grandma, on the other
hand, instead of saying, "Of course, you can't run away," listens to Susan, without agreeing with her act of defiance, and
practices a technique that psychologists call *feedback*. It is so
effective and so simple that I wish I had learned about it years
ago. It would have saved a lot of frustrations.

"You're running away because you're mad at your mother.
Is that right, Susan?"

"She's mean."

"Is your mother mean because she won't let you go over to
Karen's this late in the afternoon?"

No response. By this time Susan is beginning to lose enthusi-
asm for her escape from home, and Grandma realizes it's time

for a diversionary tactic. "Come on, honey, let's go make a salad for supper. You can help me."

In his book, *Becoming a Grandparent,* Dr. Fitzhugh Dodson says, "The purpose of the feedback technique is to express to a child that you understand how she feels. Superficial responses such as 'I know just how you feel' and 'I felt the same when I was your age' will not do the trick."

Here's what Dr. Dodson recommends:

1. Listen carefully to what the child is telling you.
2. Put the child's feelings into your own words and feed them back to her.

So much of our time is spent in talking to children, that we miss the wonderful experience of listening to what they have to say. When you listen to a child, you temporarily become a child again, entering into his magical world of wonder.

Remember how the disciples tried to keep the children away from Jesus, "But Jesus said, 'Let the little children come to me, and don't prevent them. For of such is the Kingdom of Heaven' " (Matthew 19:14).

Jesus loved children. A little child is teachable, trusting, unsophisticated, and loving. That's the way He wants us to accept Him—as a child.

Hear Them Out

Children pass through stages of behavior. It's very important for us grandparents to realize that they aren't our little angels all the time and that there will be times when their behavior absolutely baffles us. Don't blame the parents, look at the age. One psychologist says that in going from stage to stage, a child moves from a stage of equilibrium to a stage of disequilibrium, and then back again. In parent and grandparent words, this simply means that the stage of equilibrium is when a child is a pleasure to be around, and the stage of disequilibrium is when he is generally obnoxious. An easy way to remember the ages and stages is to understand that the even-numbered ages, two and four, are usually times of disequilibrium, and the odd-numbered ages, one, three, and five, are times of equilibrium.

Unless we understand these changes, we may be baffled by the precious, loving little toddler who turns into the demanding little king, who gives the orders, bangs his head, and tries your patience to the utmost. The terrible twos were not named by accident.

Erin, a motherly little five-year-old, was frequently harassed by her two-year-old brother, Taylor. One day, as Taylor was nearing his third birthday, Erin had some exciting news for her grandma.

"Grandma, guess what. Taylor has a new word he's learned. It's *yes*"!

If we cuddle them and talk to them when they're babies and listen to them when they're preschoolers, we will have more of a chance to have them as our friends in their teen years.

One of my grandchildren came to me one time, complaining that her parents were unfair. "Grandma, they just expect me to do too much housework; that's the reason my grades aren't so hot. I just don't have time to study."

I heard her out, not commenting on either the low grades or her seemingly heavy demands, and then said, "Honey, let's look at your priorities. Your mom and dad are working hard, so let's figure out how you can get your chores done first and have plenty of time for homework and fun."

It wasn't a big crisis, but she knew I'd listen.

Grandchildren somehow feel their grandparents will lend that listening ear, for the grandparents have already experienced many of the same problems with their own children.

Granted, some grandchildren may think we grandparents are too old to understand their problems. But if we honestly share some of our own problems with our grandchildren, we can make a covenant to help each other.

For those of you who like to use lists for guidelines, here's a list of positive paths to listening:

1. Look 'em in the eye. I've watched Roy Rogers captivate the hearts of children everywhere by simply stooping down and giving them his full attention. It's called caring communication.
2. Try to talk to one child at a time. Grandparents, when you have more than one grandchild around, pay attention to each one.
3. Use the feedback technique. Developing feedback is simply repeating what a person has said in another way.
4. Share stories, but don't moralize.

Grandchildren appreciate us more if they feel they can talk about their problems with us. But the groundwork for such relationships grows out of our availability. This doesn't mean, necessarily, that we need to be physically close by, but it's the closeness of our interests and attitudes that count. Find out who their heroes and heroines are, learn about their hobbies and sports, and then just listen to the wonderful language of youth.

I find the young people of today interesting, exciting, challenging, and stimulating. I have no desire to sit in a rocking chair, "tsk-tsking" about the "wild young generation." I find them bright, healthily inquisitive, and just plain fun.

That leads me into the next subject. . . .

3

. . . Be Fun

"My grandpa plays dominos and checkers with me . . . mostly I win."

CARLI
Age 8

One of our grandchildren was spending the weekend with Roy and me, and I was clowning around with her in the kitchen. Suddenly she put her hands on her hips, cocked her head to one side, and stared at me. I knew one of those piercing statements that children are prone to make was forthcoming. A child has not learned the art of tact, and frequently her remarks unveil a trait or weakness in us adults that we'd rather not have exposed.

This time, however, her comments were welcome. She said, "Why, Grandma, you have fun. I thought grandmas were too old to have fun!"

Lord, help us grandparents to be young at heart with the young.

One tactic every experienced grandparent knows, if he wants to establish a warm bond with the grandchildren, is a simple one: Get rid of the parents.

I love my children and cherish the times we can be together, separately and as a family, but when we're all together, there's no opportunity for us, as grandparents, to share any of those special moments that build our relationships with the grandchildren. Somehow, we get into a massive competition for attention. Not only do the children compete, but the parents do, also. Sibling rivalry is not limited to brothers and sisters.

When children are small, some parents want them to be on their very best behavior before Grandma and Grandpa. (After all, our children need to prove what good parents they are.) So what happens to the poor kids? "Give Grandma a kiss." "Don't touch Grandma's table." "Let Grandpa have that chair." "Eat the nice supper Grandma made for you." Good grief, if the grandchildren can get through all the warnings, admonitions, and orders and still love us, they deserve a gilt-edged gold ribbon.

Whether in your home of theirs, take the opportunity to be alone with your grandchildren. If possible, take them one at a time.

Sometimes We're Crazy

Without a little child to lead us, we could become the stereotype of stodgy, cranky old persons. Sometimes we do the most ridiculous things, because our grandchildren help us shed our years.

Before we moved to our new home on the edge of the Apple Valley golf course, we had a house on Highway 18, near a fairly steep hill. Our three youngest granddaughters were visiting us for the weekend and asked if I would climb the hill with them. "Please, Grandma, could we take our lunch and eat it high up?"

Well, at my age I began to hedge, but an inner voice said, *It's never too late to enjoy grandchildren and to share this kind of experience.*

I packed four lunches, and we started out to climb the mountain. It was a challenge. We'd climb a bit and then slip back; we had to serpentine most of the way, because it was quite steep. We reached the three-quarter mark, and Grandma had to give up. We sat down, first inspecting the area very carefully for rattlesnakes. Each of us took a perch on a big rock, thanked the Lord for His blessings, and ate lunch. The panoramic view of Apple Valley was beautiful, and the girls still talk about the wonderful time we had.

Not all experiences are so positive. One Saturday afternoon I took Dusty's three children, who were thirteen, eleven, and five, to the movies. Perhaps, in some recess of my subconscious, I thought I might revive those wonderful days when Saturday-afternoon movies were exciting escapes into wholesome adventure. From the time I slipped on the popcorn-covered floor, to the revulsion I felt over some of the violent scenes, the afternoon was a disaster. The movie was about a killer shark, and the gore was so graphic that I had to hide my eyes from some of the scenes. When the man disappeared into the jaws of the shark, I couldn't look. It actually made me nauseous.

However, I did learn something from that afternoon. Children are so used to seeing violence on television that when they go to the movies, they are conditioned to wanting more. No wonder children are so hyper.

I don't want to go back to the Dark Ages, but I don't think ours is a particularly enlightened age. We have gone a long way in technology, but these increased skills have outstripped our hearts.

Positive Alternatives

A friend of mine has initiated a Saturday afternoon at the movies at her house. She and her husband purchased a movie projector, and they rent full-length features or borrow them from the library. They are having a marvelous time with their grandchildren and the neighborhood children, not only with some of the old classics, but discovering adventure and motivational films, also.

Roy and I are beginning to build a library of video cassettes, so when the grandchildren come over we can show films of the family.

With so many movies being put onto video cassettes these days, with some discrimination over the choice, we could put Saturday-afternoon movie time back on the calendar—in the home.

Eyes in the Back of Your Head

When your grandchild is a toddler, having fun is just a watching game. This is the time when grandparents and little ones may have some difficulties. One of the things we need to realize is that we must childproof our homes at this stage. Of course, I believe in teaching a child not to touch, but if we are going to develop a nervous rash over valuable crystal within reach of tiny hands, then put the crystal away. Seems so simple, and yet I've watched grandmothers become absolute wrecks when little ones come to visit.

The first Thanksgiving in our new Apple Valley home could have been a disaster, but the Lord had His guardian angels around our grandkids. While the women were busy in the kitchen and the men were occupied with conversation, some of the children were playing hide and seek. Our house is fairly large, and there are a lot of nooks and crannies in which to conceal oneself.

Roy won't allow the children to chase up and down the stairs, so there were frequent shouts of, "You stop runnin' now." Finally everyone seemed to simmer down and relax. After a short time we started counting noses and discovered that a couple of the children were missing. We began to search in every room and closet; I went into the master bathroom, and there they were, two little monkeys curled up on the wooden slats, with the heavy glass doors closed on our recessed cubicle, which is called an environmental panel. One twist of a knob, and they might have been scalded. I hauled them out and said, none too gently, "You are never to come in here without my permission, do you understand?" They understood.

Let me explain an environmental panel. When our house was being designed, our son Dusty, who was the builder, suggested we build in this amazing "closet" to help our aches and pains and generally relax us. It can be programmed to simulate chinook winds, spring rain, sunshine, or steam. A computer regulates the length of time for these weather conditions. (I must admit I don't use it much myself, because of the rampage it creates with my hair.)

Anyhow, the grandchildren can use it, but only with strict supervision. We also have a sunken tub in that bathroom, with a Jacuzzi in it. That's off limits, too, because of the wild splashing that goes on. I believe in allowing the children to have fun, but I don't think children should wreck Grandma and Grandpa's home.

Safety First, Not Last

One of the greatest dangers lurking in every house is the caustic household cleaner or chemical. Those drain cleaners, for instance, that contain lye, have caused more children's deaths than any other household product. Buy locks for cupboards or those easy-to-install latches that can be placed inside a cupboard door. An adult can open the door and undo the latch, but a child cannot.

It only takes a little time to put high bolts on the inside of doors leading to stairways or to outside doors.

Buy a car seat, and be sure your grandchild is secure in it; never leave him unattended in a bathtub or around a pool of water. I heard of one case where a three-year-old drowned in a fishpond while his grandmother was on the telephone.

After you have taken the proper safety precautions, then you may have fun observing the wonderful world of toddler exploration. If his special world is (almost) accident proof and you have provided him with some toys to work off his excess energy, then you will have a marvelous time. And so will he.

If you are not physically or mentally able to cope with life in a monkey cage, have an older child come over and play with your little Tarzan or Jane, while you supervise from a chair. Martyr crowns do not fit a grandmother or grandfather's head.

Time to Be Messy

Close your eyes, Grandma and Grandpa, Tommy is two and a half and changing from toddler to little boy. He loves to play with sand, dirt, Play-Doh, and paints. If we fuss at the mess, we'll miss the fun!

Taking a grandchild out to a restaurant at this age is not my idea of fun. He's too big for a high chair, too small for good manners, and leaves a trail of crackers, spilled milk, and disaster in his wake. Your idea of a good time may be dinner out, but his idea is dinner all over everything.

What can we do with these children? First of all, we should gear the fun to their age and not try to push them forward into activities that are too long or too demanding. Get large sheets of paper (or use newspapers) and provide them with water-soluble paint and large paint brushes. Buy very large crayons that are easy to handle.

Did you ever try giving your small grandchild a bucket of water and a large brush and allowing him to "paint" outside? That's an absorbing occupation—for a short time.

One grandmother told me about a children's soap that contains nontoxic colors and can be painted on the skin. The child has long bath sessions when he makes up like a clown and comes out squeaky clean. The mess is a blessing.

A Time to Go Places

Hallelujah! They're toilet trained, can talk with reasonable intelligence, and eat in a more civilized manner! Before they begin school, our grandchildren are usually interested in doing things with us and going places. We are ready to plan little trips or special visits. Of course, we can't generalize about children, because they are unique individuals and do not comply to a pattern, but in general they enjoy going.

Preschoolers are wonderful at telling it as it is. Generally, they will express their thoughts and feelings very freely to us. When they get a little older, they will only tell their peers their innermost thoughts. So let's enjoy them in those few fleeting years when they are willing to jabber our ears off!

There are two things we should remember in the process of having fun with our preschool grandchildren. First, they have a very limited attention span. Imagine a scene like this: Grandma promised Kathy a trip to an amusement park. Both are ready to go when the phone rings. This is someone Grandma had been waiting to hear from, and the conversation takes a few minutes. To Kathy, it seems like an hour. At her age, patience is not a virtue; it's an unknown trait. So don't expect it. The second thing that will contribute to our fun process is planning. We should plan games, stories, physical activities. Let's be creative, grandparents, and discover the wonderful fun of childhood (even if some people call it our second childhood).

The Grand Embarrassment

Our grandson Robbie was a real caution as a youngster. We had a stone wall around our house on Highway 18, and he had been told not to walk on it. Defiantly, he was teetering on top when Roy told him to get down, in a tone that meant business.

"I don't have to," replied Robbie.

Grandpa Roy marched over to our apple tree and broke off a small branch, stripping it down to make a switch. Robbie watched him with some degree of apprehension, but was saved by the phone ringing. Roy went to answer it, and when he returned, Robbie had broken the switch in five pieces. He didn't get away with this maneuver, however; he had to get down.

This same Robbie expressed himself on nationwide television, to the chagrin of mother, Linda, and the amusement of a few million viewers.

It was Jonathan Winters' big Christmas program on CBS, and the entire Rogers family made an appearance. We were all prepared for the final dress rehearsal that was performed before a live audience. The big part of the program featured Winters doing his famous Uncle Neddy Nordic skit. He was the star, and it was his funniest scene; at least, he thought it was to be his scene.

Just as Winters really got into his character, Robby spied a ball, ran for it, and walked in front of Winters, bouncing the ball through his entire monologue. We snapped our fingers at Robby, whispered to him, and tried everything to get him back into position. Winters was furious over being upstaged, but kept his cool and was magnificent in his controlled frustration.

When the rehearsal was over, the people producing the show came on stage and said, "That's the funniest scene we've ever seen—we're going to print the dress rehearsal."

Robbie was an instant star, in spite of the embarrassment of his family.

Today Robbie's energies in his parents' church, where his father is minister, are channeled toward a Christian music ministry. It all started with a bouncing ball.

Songs and Words

One of the things I always loved to do with my grandchildren was to sing songs and repeat nursery rhymes I could remember! Beginning to read to them at this stage is marvelous, especially when you can cuddle up in a large chair and share some of the wonderful stories they love to hear repeated over and over. It's never too early to begin Bible stories and prayers.

The great preacher of the past century, Charles Spurgeon, wrote this:

> When to Start
> Ere a child has reached to seven
> Teach him all the way to heaven;
> Better still the work will thrive
> If he learns before he's five.

Time to Be a Character

One grandmother I knew was not physically able to take her granddaughter shopping or do any vigorous activities, but she provided fun by just "being a character." She brought out her harmonica and played "Old MacDonald Had a Farm"; she regaled her granddaughter with stories of her own childhood. Many years later, that granddaughter told me she remembered how her grandmother would put her tongue through her false teeth and make them wiggle. Grandmother was fun because she deliberately put on a show of being a character.

Some of my grandchildren think of me as a character, and I don't mind in the least. In fact, I rather enjoy that reputation, because it indicates a certain bemused indulgence on their part. As they grow older, I would hope for our relationships to turn into friendships.

There are so many children in the world who lose out on

fun. For the ones God gave to us, let's try to make the moments we have with them filled with as much joy as we are capable of giving.

A brilliant, talented blind pianist, Ken Medema, wrote a poignant song entitled, "Lover of the Children." It's just meant for all of us grandparents.

Walking in the sunshine—laughing in the rain
Lover of the children, make me young again.
Climbing in the treetops—running down the shore
Lover of the children, make me young once more.
Vigorous and daring—teachable and mild
Lover of the children, make me like a child.
Trusting in your goodness—walking where you lead,
Lover of the children, make me young, indeed.
Make me young enough to know that alone I cannot go
    in the darkness of the night
Make me young enough to see that your love will never
    Let me go.
Make me open to surprise, put wonder in my eyes.
    Make my vision clear and bright.
Make me willing to be led—and to follow where you bid me go.
    Fearing not tomorrow, trusting You today.
    Lover of the children, make me young, I pray.

Amen and amen for us grandparents! I have recorded and used this song in many gospel concerts across the country. Unless we can remember and cherish the joys of our own childhood, it is almost impossible to understand our grandchildren.

4

... Build a Treasure House of Memories

"Before he was handicapped, Grandpa used to take
me to parks. Now he can't, so I visit him."
"What do you do for him?"
"I just kiss him."

JENNIFER
Age 10

When Jennifer was asked in her Sunday-school class what
she liked to do with her grandma and grandpa, she made the
beautiful comment above.

What do we want from our grandchildren? Just what Jennifer had to give: love.

Memories last long after the toys and trinkets are broken.

One of my fondest memories is of the mulberry tree in my
Grandfather Wood's front yard in Uvalde, Texas. How I loved
climbing that tree, reaching out to stuff a handful of warm
mulberries into my purple-stained mouth. There were so many
wonderful things to do at Grandfather Wood's.

In the backyard there was a creaking windmill, with a wire
stretching from the top platform down to the garden gate. A
hollowed-out metal pipe, about a foot long, was strung on the
wire. I can remember filching a few cold biscuits from the
kitchen and climbing to the high platform on the windmill.
Then I would grab the pipe with one hand, and holding the
cold biscuit in my other hand to grease the wire, I would slide
down to the garden gate.

I hit the ground running and stopped right in front of the gate. I can't remember how I got the metal pipe back to the top platform, but the procedure of sliding down is indelibly etched in my memory. My grandfather did not prohibit this enjoyment, and I loved him for it.

Grandfather Wood was tall, with an angular build, and could eat like a horse without putting on a pound. If any of us grandchildren were finicky in our appetites, he could challenge us to race and finish the food on our plates.

His bedroom was in the center of the rambling ranch-type home, with a huge fireplace dominating the room. He was a great one for fruit for health, and he kept a big barrel of fruit from the Rio Grande valley on a table in his room. Each night at bedtime all of us (grownups included), would be summoned to Granddaddy's bedroom for prayer and fruit. He was an avid Bible reader and based his life on the truths of God as contained in His Word.

Granddaddy was a Rotarian, and I can still remember the huge Christmas tree Rotarians decorated in the town square. There was a small gift for every child in town; the place was jumping with excited children.

When my teeth obviously needed braces, it was my grandfather who furnished the money for the orthodontist's work.

He was the most thoroughly honest man I have known. His word was strictly his bond; one never needed a written contract with my grandfather. He believed in selling off one's coat, if necessary, to pay one's debt.

Grandfather was very affectionate. I loved visiting him and considered it an extreme privilege to go to the "picture show" with him. My grandmother had died, and he missed her terribly. I'd watch him in the movies, and about halfway through, he would nod and drift off into sleep. It puzzled me. I would stroke his arm and ask, "Granddaddy, why do you go to the picture show and then go to sleep before it's over?"

"Honey," he'd explain, "since your grandmother went away, I get very lonely for romance, and the romance on the screen is all I have left. I guess that's the main reason I go to the picture show."

Of course, those were the days when romance was romance, and not pornography.

I'm sure Grandfather Wood gave me other presents, in addition to braces, but I can't remember them. What I do remember were the prayers before each meal, the strength of his character, and the things we did together.

Impressions when children are small may last all their lives. I was only seven years old when my grandmother Wood died, yet I can remember her sitting on the back porch in that little Texas town, churning butter, singing hymns, and reading her *Baptist Standard.*

When she was very ill in the hospital, I visited her and rubbed her arms to help her circulation. I said, "Mama Wood, do you hurt real bad?" She looked at me with such peace in her face and said, "It's all right, honey; the Lord's with me."

Today Will Be Tomorrow's Memories

In reading what wise King Solomon said in Ecclesiastes, I was impressed that he had tried every avenue of pleasure and found everything futile. He wrote:

> For what does a man get for all his hard work? Generations come and go but it makes no difference. The sun rises and sets and hurries around to rise again. The wind blows south and north, here and there, twisting back and forth, getting nowhere. The rivers run into the sea but the sea is never full, and the water returns again to the rivers,

and flows again to the sea . . . everything is unutterably weary and tiresome. No matter how much we see, we are never satisfied; no matter how much we hear, we are not content.

                                                    Ecclesiastes 1:3–11

So many people live their lives as Solomon describes: with futility. As we grow older, if we feel that what we do or what we say makes no difference, then we are missing out on the true meaning of our existence. Solomon, after all his self-examination and pleasure-seeking ways, discovered how life could have real purpose. He said:

Here is my final conclusion: fear God and obey His commandments, for this is the entire duty of man. For God will judge us for everything we do, including every hidden thing, good or bad.

                                                    Ecclesiastes 12:13, 14

What does this have to do with being a grandparent? Plenty. God gave us our children and our grandchildren as extensions of His love. He holds us responsible for how we treat those gifts. Solomon also says, "Give generously, for your gifts will return to you later" (Ecclesiastes 11:1).

When children miss the grandparent relationship, they miss one of the richest bonuses that life can offer. This goes for the grandparent, as well.

Never Too Old

A favorite grandmother memory was told by a man whose boyhood ambition was to be a pilot. He worked long, arduous hours, shoveling sand from filter beds at the local sanitary plant. It was an unsavory job, but he needed money for flying lessons.

Each week he put aside his small salary and accumulated enough to pay for the hours of ground school and flying experience he needed. When he received the coveted private license, he wanted to take someone flying. His father shook his head, "Not with my high blood pressure." His mother became ill at the thought. However, his eighty-year-old grandmother, who had never been up in an airplane, said, "Why don't you ask me, Jimmy? I haven't had a good thrill for years." Grandma was the only one in the family who would share Jimmy's dream, and as he grew older he told and retold the story of Grandma Elsie, shouting against the engine's roar, "This is the most fun I've ever had; let's go again."

Never Too Busy

One of our granddaughters, who graduated from the Bible Institute of Los Angeles, demonstrated her need of this relationship, to the extreme joy of her grandfather, Roy Rogers. I asked her if she had any particular thing she wanted as a graduation gift, and she promised to think about it and let me know. A few days later, she called and asked for "Grandpa Roy," telling him she had just one fond wish for graduation.

She said shyly, "Grandpa Roy, I want you to take me hunting."

This was a complete surprise to us, because she had started out a music major, like her father, Tom, and changed in midstream to education. To my knowledge, she had never shown an interest in hunting, although she was quite active as a cheerleader in high school. (I'm not quite sure what that analogy means, except that they both take a certain amount of athletic ability.)

Roy was visibly touched by her request and joyfully complied. First she broke a clay pigeon and was ecstatic over her aim. Later she got her pheasant. Roy donated one of his, and I told her how to cook them. A week or so later, she wrote a beautiful letter of thanks, asking if he would take her again sometime. Here is her letter:

Dear Grandpa Roy,

I want to thank you so much for the "bestest" present I've ever gotten. Beside the excitement of learning to shoot a gun, watching the dogs work and later even cooking a pheasant, my most favorite part was being with you, just you without a crowd. I guess I enjoy being comfortable when you feel comfortable. I wish I would have caught on to the fact that you're a neat grandpa about twenty years ago, when I was hiding in closets from you! I couldn't think of adequate words to thank you so I drew this picture for you, because I want you to know there is something about a grandpa that no one else can copy. Spending time together with you meant more to me than any other present you could buy. I really felt loved ... and love is the most precious gift I can think of to give anyone.

I love you, Grandpa.

JULIE

Later, Julie confided to me that what she wanted most of all was to really know Roy in a one-to-one relationship. Her maternal grandfather passed away when she was quite young, and even though she had two loving grandmothers, she had missed the grandfather relationship.

Things to do, places to go, these are not always our responsibility, grandparents. Let the children come up with their ideas. Give them the boundaries of your energy, your time, or your money, and allow them to be creative. You'll never know what fun it is to have a child lead you, until you're willing to follow!

5

. . . Create a Tradition

"My grandmother reads to me all the time because she has lots of books that belonged to my dad."

CARRIE

Age 7

Tradition has a solid sound to it, but it can also carry the impression of being old fogyish or obsolete. I believe that certain traditions should be memory links to bind together the generations. The standard for a good tradition should be one that is fun and voluntary. Being forced into a traditional mold could be a divisive, rather than a cohesive tactic.

Holidays and special occasions are usually the events that make traditions. Thanksgiving Day is our one big family day. It's the only day we have any chance of getting the entire Rogers clan together. The house jumps with activity, and if I have a chance to sit down for fifteen minutes, I'm lucky. But I love it. My daughters and daughters-in-law help in the kitchen, and we all have a great time stumbling over each other and the children.

I do the big cooking on that day, and the girls contribute casseroles and desserts. We had forty-four at our last Thanksgiving dinner. Roy looked around at the crowd and said, "Ma, look what we started!"

Our Thanksgiving is traditional, with the children, grandchildren, and sometimes great-grandchildren coming to our house. Many families are not able to recreate that old custom. Houses are too small, grandparents live far away or would rather eat at a restaurant than make a three-day chaos in the kitchen. There are other ways to create memorable traditions.

One grandmother began a tradition at Christmas time, which had a lasting effect upon her grandchildren. She put special Christmas ornaments on the tree for the grandchildren, and they took them home to begin their own collection of ornaments. Another grandmother made each of her grandchildren an afghan.

Traditions are created by a consistent act, no matter how large or small it may be.

Traditions are wrapped up in visits. Either the grandchildren are visiting us, or we are visiting them. From talking to grandparents around the country, I believe many of us need to learn the art of visiting. If there is an art in conversation, an art in dressing, and an art in just about every other conceivable act, certainly there is an art in visiting. The proverb says:

> By wisdom a house is built,
> And by understanding it is established;
> And by knowledge the rooms are filled
> With all precious and pleasant riches.
> Proverbs 24:3, 4 NAS

All Together Now

The big visit, when the family all gathers at one house for a major celebration, can be a mixed bag of joy and frustrations. The joy comes from the anticipation of seeing the children again or from watching the grandchildren in their new stages of growth. However, the frustration may arise when conversations are too brief, when precious moments are stolen by the sheer work of preparing and cleaning up after a big meal.

How can we make that all-important *big occasion* be one

where the memories we build are woven into beautiful traditions?

When the crowd all tumbles into Grandma and Grandpa's house, it's time for some ground rules. Grandma would be smart to have precious vases and fragile plants put away for the day. Better yet, hurt feelings, martyr complexes, and impatient remarks should be stored. If we plan for confusion and exhaustion, we won't be surprised when we receive what we anticipated!

A child will never remember how tidy our houses looked, but he will always remember how neat his grandmas were.

Visiting the Kids

An Irish proverb says, "The eye should be blind in the house of another." That should be written for grandparents who visit their children and grandchildren. For a long-distance grandparent (one who is far enough away that he must stay overnight or longer) there should be some time to get ready for that visit.

Sometimes the family doesn't think it's important to prepare for one another because, "They're just family, not company." If more of us treated family like company and company like family, we would be known for warm, hospitable homes.

Grandparents, be considerate of the time you choose to visit. If you are coming in by plane, pick an hour when it is convenient to be met at the airport. Or if you can afford it, rent a car for your own transportation. Check with your own children about sleeping accommodations. Take a nearby hotel if you have to move grandchildren from their beds or make them double up.

One set of grandparents brought their motor home and parked it in the driveway. They could retreat to their own little domain, but be on hand for meals and fun times. In fact, in this instance, Grandfather arrived with tools and work clothes to help his son build an addition on his house.

One of the perils in visiting is upsetting the routine of the household. One mother said, "It took three weeks for us to get back to normal after my parents went home."

What happened to cause this mini trauma? A series of little things: Not knowing the rules of the house, failing to understand the importance of consistent discipline, and sugar were the most disruptive issues.

We could all learn from those remarks, grandparents. We should leave the discipline to the parents, but when we are left alone with the little sweethearts, know what their moms and dads expect of them—and us. If the children are supposed to go to bed at 7:30 and we let them stay up to 9:00 "just while we're here," we've placed some sand in the household gears.

What are the disciplinary methods used? If they are different from those we used, Grandma and Grandpa, then we should glue our lips and follow the lead of our children. They are the parents now; we had our chance on them, for better or for worse, and it's their turn to do the honors.

Did I say *sugar?* Please understand that I don't always follow these marvelous admonitions that I toss around with such pontifical ease. The sugar syndrome is one of them. However, I would just like to repeat some of the accusations I have heard from young parents. "When my folks are around, my kids get more sweets than I ever give them. It takes me weeks, sometimes, to get them away from teasing for cookies or candy."

When I was younger there wasn't the emphasis upon nutrition that we hear today. We grew up with the abundance of cakes and pies that represented hours of loving work. We bought penny candy out of the big jars in the store and stuffed our molars with gum drops and cavities. However, we also had fresh vegetables and tree-ripened fruit, which many in this era find difficult to buy. This generation of young people has become very conscious of some of the evils of sugar, yet we grandparents persist in the sweet syndrome.

One grandfather, visiting his children and grandchildren for a few weeks, loved to pick his grandson up from nursery school and walk home with him. Every day about 11:30 A.M. they had to pass the ice-cream store. "Just one little ice-cream cone won't hurt him," Grandpa said. It took a week before his mother discovered why little David wouldn't eat his lunch.

If there is anything we can do when visiting our grandchildren, it's to think before we speak. One grandmother said shortly after she arrived at her daughter's house, "Honey, I can't resist giving advice. Forget it and go do what you want." Whenever she slipped and handed out some suggestions, she managed to laugh at her relapse, and so did her daughter.

We may forget simple things when we visit. For instance, children are fascinated by grown-up talk and gossip. We should be careful what we say when they are around. One grandmother I know said that she could remember, as a child, lying on the floor, with her ear on a heating vent that went into the living room. She could hear what the adults were saying when they thought she was taking a nap.

Another question of the household, which may be taboo, is money. When grandparents come to visit, who pays for what—and how? One way to circumvent the grocery problem is just take the list and go shopping yourself. Or invite your grandchildren's parents out to dinner and offer to pay for the baby-sitter, too!

Grandparents still feel like parents to their children and should have the pleasure of giving them a surprise check. On the other hand, one married daughter told me, "I would never think of paying for groceries when we go to visit my parents. That would insult them."

Off to Grandma's House

When the grandchildren visit, then grandparents' home rules apply. Some of my grandkids started jumping on our king-size bed, pretending it was a trampoline. I said, "Look here, this is not allowed in my house. Jumping on the bed is out, understand?" They understood. We have rules of the house, and when they come, they obey them.

Young people are very adaptable. We have a big living room, and when a bunch of the grandchildren arrive, they may spread all over the floor in sleeping bags. The important thing is, how flexible are we? Are we prepared for the fingerprints on the hall mirror, the crackers ground into the carpet, or jam on the living-room couch? Does the sight of clothes dropped in the bathroom or shoes lost under the kitchen table drive us up a wall? If we are extremely finicky about our home, then it might be better not to invite the grandchildren over or to change our ways.

Personally, I know heaven is going to be a wonderful place, immaculate and perfect in every way. If our houses get a little messy on earth, it's worth it.

Some ideas for grandmothers and grandfathers to consider if they are expecting a fun-filled time:

Find out the eating and sleeping schedules.
Have a list of favorite foods.
Know the rules that you should enforce.
Be flexible, but make plans for activities.

Pass Them On

One young father recalled a family tradition that he intends to continue as soon as his children are old enough. Beginning December first, each day the family memorized a verse from the Christmas story in Luke. At supper time, they would recite the verse together. On Christmas morning, with the entire passage memorized, they repeated that beautiful story from memory, before opening presents.

So many traditions in families center around holidays, and also around food. Even if we're not fabulous cooks, I think it's a great idea to have a reputation for at least one outstanding dish and to serve that on special occasions. Writing down a recipe and giving it to a grandchild provides a lasting memory every time that little card is pulled out of the recipe box.

In our family, Christmas is a time when Roy and I believe the grown children should be starting traditions in their own homes. Since some of our family lives nearby, we have a Christmas celebration at our house early in the month, complete with dinner and gifts. Then on Christmas Day we go house hopping from one family to another. This gives the grandchildren an opportunity to have their worship and gift giving in their own homes.

Today we are experiencing a return to nostalgia. Homes are being decorated in the manner of years past. Styles are reflecting the old-fashioned look: prairie dresses, boots, pinched waists, and leg-of-mutton sleeves. It appears that we are trying to make a statement for the times. When life is so uncertain, morality on such a decline, why not try to hang on to some of the beautiful, stable elements of the past?

Traditions are:

Grace said at meals
Repetitious jokes, with predictable punch lines
Warm cornbread and fresh strawberry ice cream
A patchwork quilt passed from mother to daughter
Old tools, carefully mounted in a shadow box
Cranberry jelly, not from a can
Toys stored in the same corner of the closet

Dolls wrapped in tissue, waiting for granddaughter's fourth
birthday
Silly games known only to the players
Photo albums and yellowed newspaper clippings
The *National Geographic* piled in the corner of the attic

Traditions may be man-made or God inspired. The Bible
says, "See to it that no one takes you captive through hollow
and deceptive philosophy, which depends on human tradition
and the basic principles of this world rather than on Christ"
(Colossians 2:8 NIV).

When the lead character, Tevye, sang "Tradition" with such
gusto in *Fiddler on the Roof*, he was echoing Old Testament
principles. Traditions are based on the Bible, and God established the precedent.

Remember what happened to Joshua when he was leading
the Israelites across the Jordan River? They were carrying the
Ark of God and preparing for the last stage of the journey into
the Promised Land. But the Jordan River was overflowing its
banks, and none of the Jews had their Red Cross certificates.

God had promised Joshua that He would perform a great
miracle. The first priest touched his dusty sandal to the water's
edge; the river stopped flowing and piled up as though against
an invisible wall. Just as their forefathers crossed the Red Sea
forty years before, the Israelites walked across on dry ground.

God told Joshua to build two monuments of twelve stones
each, one at the location of their campsite, the other in the
middle of the Jordan River. Why? To establish a traditional
memorial site.

Joshua told the people:

In the future, . . . when your children ask you why these
stones are here and what they mean, you are to tell them
that these stones are a reminder of this amazing mira-

cle—that the nation of Israel crossed the Jordan River on dry ground!

Joshua 4:21, 22

Grandparents, God told us to start traditions. He said:

You must love him with all your heart, soul, and might. And you must think constantly about these commandments I am giving you today. You must teach them to your children and talk about them when you are at home or out for a walk; at bedtime and the first thing in the morning.

Deuteronomy 6:5-7

One of our traditions is the family altar. We have this in our home—not as an outward symbol of piety, but as an inward need for His strength. As you walk in the front door at the home in Apple Valley, there is a stand with an old family Bible in the entryway. On the altar are two little lamps that one of my best friends gave me and a cross from Dusty's oldest daughter, Shawna. An incense burner reminds me of the Psalm: "May my prayer be counted as incense before Thee . . ." (Psalms 141:2 NAS).

In all honesty, I've not observed an obvious altar in the home of any of our children or grandchildren, but I was pleased to hear Todd Halberg, my granddaughter Candy's husband, say that he plans to build a basement study where he and Candy can retreat and have prayer and Bible study together.

We plan our estates to avoid heavy taxes; we make our wills to provide for our family survivors, knowing that dollars may be eroded by inflation or unwise investments.

Money can be spent, folks, but traditions are inherited.

6

... Comfort the Wounded

"My grandmother always listens to my problems."

HEIDI
Age 7½

The injuries may be minor when our grandchildren are young: a scraped knee, a bumped head, a denied request. Every grandparent knows what to do in these circumstances. We hold the sobbing one, fix the injured place, and kiss away the tears. That's the warm and wonderful experience of grandparenting. As the children grow, the wounds become deeper, and our roles may become more important than the person who is the keeper of the Band-Aids.

Flunked

All of us flunk at some time. Whether it be a case of not making the football team, being passed by for cheerleader, or losing a boyfriend to the school beauty queen, life's disappointments are hard to take at the time. To bear one another's burdens is a privilege, as long as we remember that the Lord is the final person to carry the load. A good grandparent is available to be a sounding board or a warm shoulder.

In the early days of my show-business career I was pursuing the desire for fame and recognition at a dizzy pace. I see a lot of young women today, divorced and struggling as single parents to raise children and keep their heads above water. I know it isn't easy. I was married when I was very young and had a baby boy to support after his father left us. My priority in life at that time was my career, and I drove myself in the relentless desire for recognition.

Tom's grandmother, my mother, was a solid, supportive help during those years and until her death in 1976. One time I fell apart, physically and emotionally, while trying to break into the Chicago show business. I wired my folks for money, and my little boy and I went home to Texas, on a train, miserable and defeated. If it hadn't been for the love of my folks and the way in which my mother took care of Tom, I don't know where we would have landed.

I believe Mom enjoyed her grandson more than she did my brother and me. She poured herself into Tom, and all her God-given and time-tested values were taught to him. Today Tom is a fine, responsible Christian husband, father, and grandfather, and it was because of Grandmother Smith and her example.

Please, I didn't mean to neglect my father. He took time with Tom, also. When he died in the spring of 1954, we went to his funeral, in Italy, Texas. As we drove the family car to the Waxahachie cemetery I glanced at Tom and saw tears flowing down his cheeks. He said, "There goes the only real father I ever knew when I was growing up."

Grandparenting is different in changing times. Today one out of every eight kids in the United States lives in a single-parent home. The trend, according to sociologists who chart the demographics of populations, indicates that four out of ten children born in the 1970s will live in single-parent homes. That's a shocking statistic when we realize the difficulty, the heartache, the strain that comes from raising children without two parents, or imagine the confusion caused in young lives when they spend part of the time with Mommy and part of the time with Daddy.

What can grandparents do in the case of a family split? The

first thing seems obvious to me: that is to counsel the couple to stay together and work it out, if possible. The Bible says:

> Now for those who are married I have a command, not just a suggestion. And it is not a command from me, for this is what the Lord himself has said: A wife must not leave her husband. But if she is separated from him, let her remain single or else go back to him. And the husband must not divorce his wife.
>
> 1 Corinthians 7:10, 11

Today we have so many Christians playing loose with God's commands. They say, "Yes, but there are certainly circumstances where divorce is necessary."

If a husband or a wife isn't a believer and leaves his or her Christian mate, then the Bible says, ". . . The Christian husband or wife should not insist that the other stay . . ." (1 Corinthians 7:15).

Whether right or wrong, many Christians are divorcing today. If counseling hits upon deaf ears and the separation is final, grandparents are in a precarious position.

It's almost impossible to have neutrality in the heart, but it's important to be outwardly neutral. Bad-mouthing one or the other of the marriage partners has started some of the most bitter and lasting rifts, to say nothing of the damage done to the children.

Death and divorce carry similar emotions, and sometimes I'm not sure which is worse. I've experienced both and know the sickening shock waves they cause.

When my music-composer husband and I split up, it was a case of Hollywood careers causing two ambitious people to go their separate ways. We didn't have children born to us, and God was not within our lives. We were like so many young couples today, blindly pursuing that elusive quality called success and not succeeding in the most important areas of our lives.

Roy and I have been married over thirty-four years now, and I never intend to get a divorce. I made that promise to God. Of course, we have had disagreements, and we've argued over important and trivial issues; but when we married, it was till death do us part, and that's that.

Yes, we have had divorce in our family, and I know the emotions a mother and grandmother have in such cases. However, I know I can't bear the hurts and disappointments for my loved ones; I can only be available when they need me.

In case of a bitter divorce, where children are often the pawns of battling parents and used for the parents' selfish reason of wanting to hurt each other, grandparents can be a soothing presence in a disturbed child's life. They can be a haven for an unfortunate child emotionally torn between two parents. This is no small task; it's like walking a tightrope when we try to establish the confidence in the child that both parents love and need him or her.

One grandmother told how her little grandson asked her, "What happened to my old dad?" She said her stomach tied up in knots trying to think how to answer the child, whose father had walked out on his family. She said, "He went to live someplace else, but he still loves you."

We need to pray for God's guidance in explaining the divorce without incriminating either of the parents. God is the judge. Later, the child will understand as he matures. Every child is entitled to the love and concern of both mother and father. When a grandparent lets the grandchild see an emotional bias for either parent, the child begins to feel a civil war building within himself. It's not fair; the child is not to blame and should be protected emotionally.

We must strive to do our utmost to let the children know that marriage is an honorable estate and there are good marriages that last a lifetime. We should teach them that God wants them to be very slow and careful in choosing a mate and that He has the right one for them.

The divorce rate is horrendous, and it is telling on our children. We grandparents whose marriages have survived the marital storms over the years must be honest with our grandchildren. We must tell them that not one of us is perfect and that Jesus forgives our mistakes. That's what the cross is all about.

I think it's harder to face the divorce issue when the family involved is a Christian family. The guilt is oppressive on everyone's part. Jesus died to take away our sins, and the only freedom from guilt is through Him.

Death and the Child

To comfort a child when someone he loves dies is a job the Lord may give us someday. I have had it both ways: telling my children about death and having them tell me. A child seems to understand more about heaven than adults, and describing the beautiful place his loved one is in can be done as graphically and with as much glorious imagination as you wish. I do believe that heaven is a wonderful place, and every child should be brought up to believe that.

I wrote in *The Woman at the Well*: "We cannot run from death, and its partings. We cannot run from anything. The sooner we accept the fact of death, and the sooner we resolve to work it out with the help of the Lord, the sooner we conquer it."

Stick Together

Sometimes grandparents have to step in and play the part of parents. It's not easy to raise a family when your physical capacity is dwindling. But God will supply His strength for every situation. The important thing is to keep the family together. The Bible says: "... Otherwise, if the family separates, the children might never come to know the Lord; whereas a united family may, in God's plan, result in the children's salvation" (1 Corinthians 7:14).

All the admonitions in the world will do no good if we aren't comforted ourselves. I find the Psalms one of the greatest sources of comfort. Absorb them, meditate upon them, pass them on.

> Lord, you are my refuge! Don't let me down! Save me from my enemies, for you are just! Rescue me! Bend down your ear and listen to my plea and save me. Be to me a great protecting Rock, where I am always welcome, safe from all attacks. ... My success—at which so many stand amazed—is because you are my mighty protector. All day long I'll praise and honor you, O God, for all that you have done for me.
>
> Psalms 71:1–3, 7, 8

7

. . . Jump the Generation Gap

"My grandma is cute."
JERED
Age 9

A child's view of age is relative to nothing. When I asked a preschooler how old a grandpa is, he answered, "Maybe twenty-three." Our grandson D. J. told his teacher that I was "eighty-six." When they're little, old is anything past thirteen; however, the generation gap widens as they get into the middle childhood years and beyond.

I believe we grandparents can do something to narrow that chasm and improve our life-styles at the same time.

The way we look at ourselves will determine how our grandchildren look at us. We have a battle to wage with today's values. In the United States we are bombarded with the glories of the young, the beautiful, and the successful.

Look at the fear many people have as they turn forty. "This is the big one," they say regretfully, as if their achievements were all in the past. We use potions, facelifts and hair coloring to stay youthful. (Not that I disapprove of looking your best.) However, in our relentless pursuit to stay young, we may convey the impression that youth has a priority on value and that growing old is a process to be avoided, at all costs. Time doesn't reverse itself; however, we can credit the aging process with more desirability than our youth-worshiping culture has been willing to give.

Growing older (not old) has a lot of advantages. Enjoy it, and your grandkids will enjoy you.

Why Be Afraid of Aging?

Not long ago I was visiting with relatives in Memphis and went to a beauty shop to have my hair done. I overheard two women discussing their grandchildren. One of them said, "Is it true you have a great-grandchild?" The other woman laughed and said quite emphatically, "Please, don't make it worse than it is! I have a new grandchild, not a great one."

I wanted to shout, "You should be so lucky, lady! I have six great-grandchildren, and it's wonderful, so don't knock it."

Why are we so afraid of age, and why do we lie about it? Whenever I am asked my age, I always flat out tell the truth. It's beautiful to reach the age where you can quit pressing to prove yourself, where you can be your own self, the person God created, with no apologies.

Yes, I try to do my best with what I have; I owe it to Roy, my friends, and myself to be well-groomed and stylish as is possible. If I only looked at the women's magazines and fashion pages, I suppose I could become despondent about this relentless march of the years; however, I look to the Scriptures and find that aging has very high priority. That's Good News.

We cannot *demand* respect, but we should *command* respect because of our love and fear of Almighty God and our example of godly living.

The Bible says: "You shall give due honor and respect to the elderly, in the fear of God. I am Jehovah" (Leviticus 19:32).

How far we have strayed from biblical principles! In the patriarchal times, the older people were the center of family life. They were the ones who gave the advice and led Israel in times of trouble. Look at the priests, the judges, and the warriors; they were admired and revered.

In Proverbs, old age is not a curse, it's a prize. "White hair is a crown of glory and is seen most among the godly" (Proverbs 16:31). In our country, the cosmetic industry sells many millions of dollars' worth of hair-coloring products.

Old age is not a burden, it's a reward. We simply need to read the instructions on this earthly package the Lord has given us. "If you want a long and satisfying life, closely follow my instructions" (Proverbs 3:2).

The best way I know of jumping the generation gap is to have the wisdom that only God can impart.

"For the reverence and fear of God are basic to all wisdom. Knowing God results in every other kind of understanding. 'I, wisdom, will make the hours of your day more profitable and the years of your life more fruitful' " (Proverbs 9:10, 11).

When our grandchildren reach those precarious preteen and teen years, only God's wisdom will suffice.

Broken Connections

Ellen's grandmother lived with them for as many years as Ellen could recall. She remembered when she was very young, around three or four, that Grandma just came to visit for long periods of time, but she had a house of her own "somewhere far away." Then one day the whole family moved to another house, and grandmother moved into her own little apartment, which was part of the main house. That was fun, because Grandma had a piano and played funny songs "by ear," she said. (Although Ellen didn't understand how she could play with her ears.) Anyhow, Grandma's adjoining apartment was a refuge from the demands of Mother. When Ellen went in the little living room and closed the door, she could share Grandma's doughnuts and Seven-Up, which she wasn't allowed to have on her side of the house. It was a secret she had with Grandma.

As Ellen grew older, she spent less time with Grandma. First, the granddaughter found her grandmother increasingly boring, and then she began to resent the intrusion in her young life when Grandma would say, "Come in and talk to me."

It's only natural that the same little boy or girl we spent hours with, playing games, going to the park, or telling stories, will come to a time when he or she would rather be with friends or watching television than chatting with Grandmother or Grandfather. Even talking to us on the telephone will be a chore, and we begin to feel pushed out of the child's life.

We feel like we've been carrying on a wonderful conversation with someone, and suddenly the wires are cut, and we're left holding a frayed memory of past fun.

If we feel injured that the little girl we cuddled now has a hands-off policy, and the little boy we cared for when he had the chicken pox, now treats us as if we had the same disease, then we are not being realistic about their age. They are breaking the bonds with their parents, too, and we need to give them time to establish communications with us on a different level.

If we have established the loving bonds when they are small, they'll come back.

Rip Tide in the Teens

It's so wonderful to watch these emerging young men and women, yet painful at the same time. They are being pulled back and forth between childhood and young adulthood, not knowing where they want to be from one day to another. They reach forward to the aspect of the big decisions, like school and career and love affairs, and yet reach back to the freedom from decisions and responsibilities that childhood offers.

What can grandparents do during these years when everything that involves the process of growing up seems "heavy, man"? If there is any advice I might give, it would be quite simple. Be available.

They may or may not want to talk about some of the weighty subjects that burden and confuse them. However, sometimes Grandma and Grandpa are more accessible than Mom and Dad. The latter have the power of punishment and disapproval, the former may disapprove, but not punish.

Harriet is the grandmother of two preschool children. She adores them and would probably pass the test as "Super Grandma" herself. She said that her greatest desire was to be the kind of grandmother her mother is. Harriet said, "My daughter is grown and is the dean in a girls' school. She calls her grandmother, long distance, and sometimes talks to her for an hour at a time. All her life my daughter has confided in and shared with my mother many aspects of her life. It's a marvelous relationship."

Who can comfort and understand better than someone who has walked the paths of life and run into the thorns and stones? The simple fact that we've lived longer, seen more, and experienced more of life's joys and sorrows should give us some advantage in being able to listen to the grandkids ventilate their problems.

Many times, as life deals us bitter blows, we groan inside, "Why me, Lord, why me?" How I love the Scripture that says:

> What a wonderful God we have—he is the Father of our Lord Jesus Christ, the source of every mercy, and the one who so wonderfully comforts and strengthens us in our hardships and trials. And why does he do this? So that when others are troubled, needing our sympathy and encouragement, we can pass on to them this same help and comfort God has given us.
>
> 2 Corinthians 1:3–5

But Mom and Dad Don't Understand

When we grandparents are the dumping ground for complaints, we need to call on God's wisdom for our reactions. We need to remember the cardinal rule: Never criticize parents to the child. We are really being tested by our grandchildren and being invited to conspire with them against their parents.

Listen to the gripes, and then take the opportunity to explain the parents to the child. When fifteen-year-old David says to Grandpa, "Dad is so unreasonable. I was a little late getting in the other night, and you'd have thought I committed a murder or something. He raved on and on about how cruel I was to Mom and how irresponsible I was and—good grief, don't they think I'm old enough to take care of myself?"

Grandpa listens and then asks David if he phoned when he knew he was going to be late.

"Gosh, I didn't want to wake them up—I was only thinking of them," David explains, with the illogical logic only a teenager seems to have.

What David isn't saying is that he didn't want to call because he didn't want to be told to come home immediately. What he didn't realize was the terrible cruelty of making parents anxious and unknowing.

Does Grandpa understand? You bet he does. He remembers when David's father pulled the same trick on him, and he can tell his grandson, with graphic illustrations of the pain that children can inflict by thoughtlessness.

Praise the Lord if your grandchildren do come to you with a line of beefs about Mom and Dad. You have built a relationship over the years that has invited these confidences. The success we have as grandparents will depend upon how tactfully we handle these sessions and how careful we are not to interfere with parental authority, unless we know that bodily harm or blatant immorality is involved. Many grandparents have become involved in situations where the lives and welfare of grandchildren were at stake. This is not a type of interference; it's loving good sense. When we see life-styles or actions that could harm our grandchildren physically or morally, then stepping in is justified, I believe. The Bible says, "Winking at sin leads to sorrow; bold reproof leads to peace" (Proverbs 10:10).

Look, folks, there's too much "winking at sin" going on today, even among Christians. It's time we establish God's authority and values, before His judgment falls upon our entire nation and every home within it.

Disappointments

I have been asked, "Did any of your children or grandchildren disappoint you?" Of course, they have, just as I have disappointed them and my own parents.

One of my children, arriving long after curfew one night, said to me, "Look, you made your mistakes, now let me make mine."

I was heartsick, believing that I had not been the model mother that she needed. I had promised God that I would influence this child to be a missionary; my heart was set on it, but it never happened.

Today, however, this child is a well-integrated young woman with a responsible job and a lovely little daughter. I had no right to plan her life for her.

Once she wrote me: "I am not an extension of you or anyone else. You will always be unhappy with me until you accept me just as I am."

When I had the grace to let go and trust her to the Lord, her life took a U-turn. All children and grandchildren must stretch and grow, and the growing can be quite painful. It was for me. The greatest assurance we have is in Proverbs 22:6 (italics mine), "Teach a child to choose the right path, and when he is *older* he will remain upon it." The emphasis is upon older. We become impatient too soon.

Disappointment is a mild way to describe my feeling when Sandy, our son, died. The ignoble way of his death was a terrible blow. However, as I think back, I am grateful that he attained his goal of private first class and that he was a Christian, in spite of the fact that he accepted a tragically ridiculous dare of hard drinking, which cost him his life.

Share Our Goofs

I was not a perfect mother. I did many things that I regret and didn't do other things I wish I had done. Many times I jumped to conclusions before hearing all the facts. Take the case of the missing knives. That was a mystery I thought I had solved, but quickly regretted my hasty solution.

On several occasions I found my favorite kitchen knives missing and after investigation found Dusty and Sandy using them to dig in the dirt or carve model airplanes. I would scold them, retrieve the knives, and ignore the infringement on my kitchen domain, until the next incident.

One afternoon I was very tired and went into the kitchen to peel potatoes for supper. My favorite knife was missing. Without a clue, I knew where to look. "Dusty," I called in my angriest mother voice, "bring me my knife immediately."

"I didn't take your knife, Mom."

I grabbed him by the shoulders and shook him, sputtering hot steam the whole time. "Young man, I am sick and tired of missing knives. You go to your room and stay there until I say you can come out."

A few minutes later I found the paring knife in the back of a drawer. However, the damage to Dusty had been done. The following Christmas he gave me a whole set of paring knives. I was humbled to the core.

Another time I couldn't find out who had done something that was an infraction of the rules, so I spanked both Debbie and Dodie. Years later Dodie told me how upset she was, because Debbie was the real culprit.

However, Roy and I loved all of our children deeply, and we know that the Lord has given us wisdom for dealing with them when we asked Him and were ready to accept His guidance.

Don't you think it's a good idea to let our grandchildren know that we weren't ideal parents, either? Perhaps they have heard some complaints about us from their parents, and that might influence their feelings toward us. However, if we talk openly about our own mistakes, we might help the grandchildren with their own relationships with their parents, our children. Teenagers, especially, have struggles with tolerance of parents. They have left the stage where Mom and Dad could do no wrong and have reached the age where Mom and Dad can do no right.

Grandparents can provide the balance that is needed to span that gap between parent and child.

We Can't Change Them

There's only one person I can change. Try as I may, I can't remake my husband, my children, my grandchildren, or my great-grandchildren. The best way I know to stay in touch with all of them, to keep the lines of communication open and to have a happy, fulfilled relationship with them is to feel like somebody myself.

We older Americans need to reinforce the fact that God loves us and gives us each new day with new hope. Sociologists have told us that people with strong religious beliefs live longer than those who have no faith. My goodness, we could have told them that, because the Bible tells us so. Proverbs says, "Reverence for God adds hours to each day; so how can the wicked expect a long, good life?" (Proverbs 10:27).

So let's feel good about ourselves and then become involved in doing something for others. Maybe we can't be like the grandparent one little nine-year-old told us about. He said, "My grandfather likes to go on the roller coaster and sit in the front seat." That wouldn't be my bag. But we can live a life that says, "Old is not awful." We can love and listen and give.

I want my grandchildren to love and trust me, to feel they can confide in me and know I will give them a straight answer. I want them to know that I love them, even though I don't always agree with, or approve of, their views or life-styles. I want them to know the Lord loves them, that He can make their lives abundant, full, rich, and satisfying.

God didn't invent the term "generation gap," man did. He said, "Encourage each other to build each other up." (1 Thessalonians 5:11).

8

. . . Spoil, If We're Not Careful

"My parents are easygoing and let me do everything I want, but my grandpa is very strict, and I'm glad. It's fun to get strict with people."

MICHELLE
Age 11

One sunny desert day I was driving my daughter-in-law, Linda, two young granddaughters, and a small grandson to a neighboring town for lunch. I had just received a beautiful silver dinner bell from my publisher, to commemorate the publishing of *Let Freedom Ring*, my bicentennial book. My gift had been unwrapped and was sitting on the floor of the car.

Enter my grandson, a superactive, bright, inquisitive little guy, who is cute as a button. (Does that sound like a grandmother talking?) D. J. grabbed the bell and began to clang it so loudly that his mother and I couldn't hear each other over the racket. One of his sisters in the backseat reached over to the front and took it from him. He was furious, and in a fit of temper, grabbed it and hit her on the head, drawing both blood and tears.

While Linda was soothing the injured one, I firmly took the bell from D. J. and announced, "That's enough! This bell belongs to Grandma, and I will have it quiet!" With that, he threw himself on the floor before the front seat, pushed my right foot on the accelerator, and pressed it to the floor. I kicked his hand off my shoe and with my right hand seized a handful of his hair, giving it a good sharp tug. He yelled like a banshee as I lifted him onto the seat beside me.

Slowing down, I put my arm around him and said, "Honey, I love you, but you cannot behave this way in my car. Your daddy wasn't allowed to do it, and you're not either." He was shocked, to say the least, but soon cooled down.

Perhaps some of you may say, "Why, Dale, surely you didn't pull your grandchild's hair?" Yes, indeed, I did, but he didn't lose any of it. He could have caused a wreck, so it was love, not the devil, that made me do it. He and I are pretty good buddies, although I admit he's so cute I have a temptation to spoil him.

That little story does not imply that I was usurping Linda's right to discipline D. J. Immediate action was needed, action strong enough to leave an impression. Intervention in this case was a necessity, due to the serious consequences of a little boy's temper.

We walk a fine line, grandparents, between loving and over-indulgence, between caring and intervention. Our guidelines need to be both common sense (and I love the book of Proverbs for some of the great one-liners of all time) and role models of other grandparents.

My Mother, My Son

I had a marvelous role model for my grandmothering years, but I didn't realize at the time that she was establishing the godly principles that I could emulate a generation later. While I was pursuing my intense youthful desires for fame in the entertainment world, Mom was playing surrogate mother to Tom. She worked hard at not spoiling Tom, and her efforts were rewarded in the evidence of his life.

Promptness is not a virtue bestowed upon us at birth. A child does not have to be taught to be late. One of the rules that my mother had was that dinner was at noon, and everyone had to be in the house, with hands washed, ready to eat when the food was served. This was not a peanut-butter-and-jelly-sandwich snack, but a real meat-and-potatoes meal. Tom would wander in after everyone had started to eat, and his grandmother would scold him; however, the next day he would be late again. Finally she said, in that tone so common to exasperated parents, "The next time you're late, I'll teach you a lesson so you won't be late anymore."

Tom was late for dinner again, and this time the punishment was due. Now I'd like to set the stage for the next scene. Imagine a small town in the 1930s. There weren't a lot of exciting events for a young boy, but the high-school football games were highlights of his existence. Every high school has its arch rival, and the game of the year was to take place on Friday night. There were banners around town; the tension was high. The winner of this game would take the conference championship.

My mother called upon her inner resources and said, "Tom, I keep my promises. I told you not to be late, and you were. You cannot go to the game Friday night."

"Mom," he wailed, "everybody's going to the game. I've been waiting all year for this. You're not going to make me stay home just for being late for dinner, are you? That's not fair."

How many generations of parents and grandparents have heard the accusation "That's not fair?" It's the national anthem for teenagers.

Well, the days marched toward Friday, with Tom becoming more vocal each hour with his protestations. "Mom [he called her Mom and me Frances until Roy and I married, when he began to call me Mother], I'll do anything, but please don't make me stay home from the game Friday night. I'll stay home for a month and never be late again. I know you don't want to be so mean."

My mother told me in later years that she never felt so terrible in her life. Other members of the family accused her of being unfair; her Aunt Octavia said, "Betty Sue, that's the cruelest thing you've ever done." It was at that point that Mother almost relented.

On the night of the game, Tom went to his room and was heard crying. Mother was in her room, wavering, too, because Tom was very precious to her. Afterwards she said, "Frances, I believed that if I gave in on that promise, Tom would never respect my discipline again. It was the hardest thing I ever did."

Tom never forgot the lesson. Today he is the most punctual person I know. He's either on time or fifteen minutes early.

There's a proverb that says: "A youngster's heart is filled with rebellion, but punishment will drive it out of him" (Proverbs 22:15).

My mother's life gave me another illustration that has stuck with me as a lesson in the potential destructiveness of gift giving. The characters are not parents and grandparents, but the principles are the same.

It was during the Depression, and every purchase was a major event. Tom's greatest Christmas desire was to have a cowboy suit. (Do you think he had some childish prophetic insight into our life to come?) My mother saved nickels and dimes, little by little, to buy her grandson the small wish of his heart. Finally she had enough saved to go to Sears and make the major purchase. It was a wonderful Christmas morning when Tom unwrapped that suit and put it on. He went outside to show the neighbor children, and one of his friends was very envious. His father was one of the fortunate people who had money during the Depression, and the boy never had to wait for his wishes; they were granted before he expressed them. Naturally he went home and described Tom's cowboy outfit, and a few days later he was outside sporting the fanciest, gaudiest suit and boots that could be purchased in the area. Tom's basement purchase looked shabby in comparison.

My mother was deflated and thought that the boy's father was insensitive in promoting the attitude of one-upmanship in his son.

That story has made me think twice about my own gift giving to my grandchildren. We may destroy the value of another's gift by our own desire to be generous.

Giving With Restraint

If grandparents have more resources than parents, it is a temptation to give the grandchildren some of the expensive and wonderful things they desire. One of the best ways to build a barrier of resentment is by giving presents that undermine parental giving ability.

How would parents feel if they had spent hours making a dollhouse for six-year-old Jeanette, hiding the project in the back of a closet, working long and loving time pasting up tiny pieces of wallpaper and cutting minute carpets, if Grandma and Grandpa invited Jeanette over to their house and presented her with s Schwarz miniature mansion, complete with Victorian furniture and crystal chandeliers?

Do you think this is an exaggeration? I heard of one grandfather who gave his two-year-old first grandson a complete Lionel train set. Another grandmother had established such a pattern of buying, with her grandchildren, that when they came to visit her, the first question was, "When do we go to the toy store?"

Grandparents, we need to examine our own motives when it

comes to gift giving. Are we doing it for our pleasure or for the benefit of the children? Naturally we give to get enjoyment ourselves, but we must not yield to the temptation of lavishness, lest we leave in our trail the injured feelings of our own children and in-laws, who will have to deal with the expensive appetites we have aroused in their children.

On the other hand, there may be the situation where parents have said there was a toy or present they couldn't afford, and the willing checkbook of Grandma or Grandpa then brings delight, not dismay. Many young families, for instance, would find the major purchase of a swing-and-slide set or a dome climber, outside the budgetary means. With the permission of the parents, this type of purchase would be a long-range investment.

Grandmothers usually are more prone to lavishness than grandfathers. Particularly in those early years, when our sons and daughters are stretching to buy playthings for their children and trying to choose those toys that are sturdy and lasting, we need to exercise careful restraint, without being stingy. This balancing act becomes steadier as we gain in grandparenting skills. It's the first-timers who have the hardest decisions.

Get Inside Information

I have news for you. Toy stores do not know the best gifts for your grandchildren; their parents do. I know a grandma who bought a puzzle with forty pieces for her five-year-old grandson, only to discover that he was working the ones with a hundred pieces. Another grandmother bought a Candy Land game for her grandchild, who had graduated to Monopoly.

After the rattle and teddy-bear stage, anything we choose as a gift is pure guesswork. It's not the kids who live with the toys

and gifts; it's their parents. Also, the parents today are more
sociologically oriented than we were. Where a set of toy sol-
diers may have been Grandpa's favorite choice for his grandson, his own son may consider them war toys. We might not
dream of choosing a doll of another race or color for our
granddaughter, and yet that might be a teaching method her
mother is using to promote the idea of good race relations.

Some Christian child psychologists tell us that the toys and
games we choose for children may have a profound influence
upon their thinking. The Barbie-doll craze, for instance, is
thought to promote a sex symbol for little girls, instead of a
mother image. I believe that toys and games are important
educational tools and should be given with wisdom and recom-
mendation of parents.

Because books and records are the greatest grandparent
gifts, I have asked a very fine compiler of information on children's books and records to list suggestions at the end of this
book. Here again, after the read-aloud stage has passed, we
need all the guidance we can get.

I was discussing with some young parents the value of reading versus television. One father said, "Since we have restricted
Jonathan's television time and rewarded him for reading, we
have discovered that he is more imaginative. He talks more
about what he wants to do and where he wants to go, whereas
before he sang the jingles from commercials."

We cannot make children read what they're not interested
in. However, if Jack is into airplanes, look for books on the
history of aviation or designs of aircraft. If Betty loves horses,
there are a wealth of books with horse themes.

Here again is where inside information is valuable. Don't
foist your interests on your grandchildren, promote theirs. A
child needs all the encouragement to read that he can get. One
grandfather bribed his high-school-age grandson to read by

offering him five dollars for every book he read and wrote a report on. In this case, Grandfather said, "Since I'm putting up the money, I get to choose every other book." The process was pure bribe, and some may not approve of the method used, but the results were that the boy entered college with better reading skills and more of an appetite for knowledge than many of his peers.

The Shopping Trips

In talking to children in the upper elementary grades, I asked, "What do you do with your grandmother that you like?" Most of the girls said, "I like to go shopping with her."

Perhaps one of the reasons they love shopping is because Grandma's purse or charge card is very handy. I think shopping trips can be made into events that are memorable, if the guidelines have been established in advance. "Today we're going to look for a graduation dress, and that's all." Or, "Let's look for a pair of slacks and a jacket for Bible camp."

One grandmother took her twelve-year-old granddaughter shopping for a special dress for a Christmas piano recital. The little girl found a black velvet outfit that was very expensive and not well made. Grandmother was in a dilemma. Should she buy the dress her granddaughter wanted, even though she didn't like it? She responded with a statement that I think is so wise in such a situation. "Honey, when I give someone a present, I like to like it, too, or I don't give it." That settled the question, and the little girl, wanting to please her grandmother, too, looked for another dress.

Men don't like shopping expeditions, as a rule, so these guidelines are aimed primarily at us grandmothers. Shopping may be spontaneous, but remember that nothing is fun when people are tired. Plan the trip for lunch or refreshments, and realize that an endurance contest is not enjoyable.

What the Children Think

A friend of mine helped me with research for this book and visited several schools and classrooms, asking similar questions. One of them was, "Do you think your grandparents spoil you?" From first graders to eighth graders, the predominant answer was, "Yes." Perhaps their impression of our loving is that of spoiling, or perhaps it's because we give them things their parents don't. But I do know that it is easy for us to do and difficult for their parents to counteract.

Another warning we need to give ourselves is about promises.

A child doesn't forget a promise made, nor does he forgive a promise broken. If we say, "If you get an A in math, I'll take you to Disneyland," then we had better produce the promised reward. Nothing is quite so crass as forgetting or ignoring that we gave our word. The Bible says: "One who doesn't give the gift he promised is like a cloud blowing over a desert without dropping any rain" (Proverbs 25:14).

Grandparents, when the sweet upturned face, framed by those unruly curls, teases for "just one more piece," when the tears roll down those smooth little cheeks after she's been sent to her room, when "everyone is going on the ski trip, but I don't have enough money," then we must remember the rule of the day: When in doubt, "Ask your mother and father."

Impartiality

Sometimes, in our efforts to be fair and impartial with our children or grandchildren, we overlook the needs of a particular child. My mother was quite upset one time when she felt one of her great-grandchildren was not treated fairly. One child had been invited to an outing but couldn't go because a younger child had health problems and had to stay home.

Mother had her say about the seeming injustice of the decision, but she was told, "Mom, you don't understand the problems."

Several years later I was faced with the same problem. I attempted to keep Debbie home from that fatal church bus trip to Tijuana because Dodie was ill and couldn't go. Debbie cried, "Mom, it isn't fair that I have to stay home because Dodie is sick." I relented, and Debbie was never to return to our home.

I try to be impartial with children and grandchildren, but it isn't always successful.

The longer I live, the less dogmatic I am in making statements like, "Treat them all the same." Children are different, and so are circumstances.

The only sameness is our oneness with Christ. He loves us equally and doesn't play favorites. The Bible says: ". . . we are all the same—we are Christians; we are one in Christ Jesus" (Galatians 3:28).

9

... Be a Surrogate Grandparent

"Life needs an objective. Otherwise the gray matter just doesn't function anymore."

GRANDMA HELEN O'ROARKE

Age 80

"Ten years ago I was all alone. My husband had died, and I sat in my little apartment with my cat, feeling sorry for myself. Then I saw an article in the newspaper about foster grandparents wanted, and I applied. Oh, my, those children are special. Now I have so much to live for."

Elizabeth is one of 18,000 senior citizens who spend four hours a day, five days a week, as a Foster Grandparent. She takes the bus every morning to a county facility for neglected and abused children. What does Elizabeth do? She loves the children, talks to them, and plays with them. Her little charges range from five to nine years of age; they all call her Grandma and look forward to seeing her every day.

Recently Elizabeth returned to her small apartment, after spending the morning playing games and helping with meals, opened her mail, and found a letter that she shows with pride to her friends. It said:

...Your dedication and devotion cannot be measured by an hourly wage, for the time and effort you give can only be reflected in the hearts of the children you so lovingly befriend.

NANCY REAGAN

Elizabeth has a new lease on life at the age of eighty-eight. When I first heard about the Foster Grandparent plan I wanted to shout hooray and bravo. This is one government-sponsored program that I'll really get behind. It was first conceived in 1965 and was given real impetus by Nancy Reagan, when her husband was governor of California. God bless her and the plan, and may it spread everywhere.

This program provides great benefits for two different groups: older, low-income people who want to participate usefully in the life of their community and to feel needed and lonely, neglected children who desperately need care, love, and attention.

Five days a week, David Paulley, seventy years old, visits Barbara, fifteen years old, a blind, brain-damaged child. Barbara is a longtime resident of the Queens Children's Psychiatric Center in New York City. "She knows my voice and footsteps," Paulley says. "She seems to be most happy when singing." What do they sing? An appropriate song, I think: "You're Nobody 'Til Somebody Loves You." Barbara ends the song with her own line: "I found myself a grandpa to love. . . ."

David Paulley is not Barbara's real-life grandparent; he is a Foster Grandparent and a special friend.

I have never heard such heartwarming stories as those told to me by these dedicated senior citizens. Sure they get paid, but the money is so little that you know they don't do it for that reason. They receive a hot meal, and eating is often the chance for learning experiences. One Foster Grandparent said many of her assigned grandchildren had never used eating utensils, but had stuffed food in their mouths like little animals.

Betty Kozasa, the director of the Foster Grandparent Program in Los Angeles, said, "The children and the foster grandparents both need what each other has to give."

Paz is a woman who raised her own eight children single-handed. She said, "We had a tough time growing up together."

Now she has sixteen grandchildren of her own, but is using her own knowledge to help kids who don't have a grandma. She volunteered to work with girls between the ages of eleven and sixteen at Juvenile Hall. These were the tough kids, wise in the ways and language of the street and suspicious of most adults. But Paz, who is bilingual, taught them Spanish cooking, how to keep a kitchen clean, and simple sanitary measures. The girls respected her, because she cared for them.

Some of the young people are delinquents who have committed every street crime, including assault and battery on old, defenseless women. Wouldn't some of the Foster Grandparents be in a dangerous position? A grandparent assigned to Juvenile Hall said, "The kids may curse and spit on the staff, but they won't with us grandparents. Sure, they test our reactions, but we're not in authority. We're on the scene to care and listen."

Give and You Will Receive

The opportunities are so abundant and the needs so glaring that no one who is physically able needs to spend his days in lonely idleness.

The Bible says, "Give generously, for your gifts will return to you later. Divide your gifts among many, for in the days ahead you yourself may need much help" (Ecclesiastes 11:1, 2).

John Regan had worked for a railroad in the accounting department until a severe heart condition forced him into retirement. He had five children and missed them so much after they left the nest. John was beginning to sink into apathy when his wife plopped a newspaper into his lap one day and pointed to an article about Foster Grandparents. "There, that ought to get you out of the chair."

John and his wife have nine grandchildren of their own, but his days were empty until he became a Foster Grandparent.

His first assignment was Freddy, a fourteen-year-old who had been in a state mental institution for the past eleven months. Freddy had his hills and valleys, with days when he would fly into uncontrollable rages and other times when he would isolate himself and not speak to anyone.

Slowly Freddy began to trust Grandpa John. The boy taught the older man to play chess. John said, "I don't know who had the most patience, but Freddy certainly had a hard time teaching this old guy a complicated game. Boy, it's good to feel that I'm needed."

It Won't Work

The world is full of negative thinkers. When the Foster Grandparent Program was launched in late 1965, the gloomsters started their black chorus. At that time it was a more prevalent attitude that retired persons had completed their usefulness, and this part of life was a time for resting. Retirement was not a right or an option, but compulsory for most. As a result, many millions of older Americans were losing financial ground because their earning power was cut off.

On the other side of the age coin were the hundreds of thousands of children in group-care institutions throughout America. They needed to be loved, wanted, and important to someone.

Today the program is not only working, it has given hope to thousands of people. It thrills me to hear some of their stories and to see the biblical principles of love and encouragement embodied in a social program.

Never Give Up

Winston Churchill made the three little words "never give up" famous in his legendary talk at West Point. There are older American citizens who are making their own history, based on those words. The story of one American hero comes from Butlerville, Indiana. Asbury Sandlin is ninety-seven years old and serving as a Foster Grandparent to a handicapped youngster at a state hospital.

On nice days, Asbury pushes his youngster in a wheelchair, showing him the trees and sky. When they go inside, Asbury just sits with his child, pats his hand, and talks to him. He says, "These kids need me. I love taking care of them. What can be better than taking care of children?"

Asbury has a little experience with children. He married a girl in Kentucky, when marrying age was really young. She was sixteen, he was nineteen, and they had eleven children. After she died, he married again and had three more children. Asbury says he has ten or twelve great-great-grandchildren (he's not quite sure).

If we went to college (and I never did), or have known some of the fine things that money can buy (and I have), what can we learn from an unschooled hillbilly who is almost a centenarian? The advice he gives young people today is, "Settle down and grow up to be nice, honorable people. Go to school. Quit drinking. A friend will try to get you to stop drinking, not start. Acting nice is better than dressing nice."

We learn from the survivors. This is one of the reasons that the older citizens have so much to offer. In the Foster Grandparent Program the average age of the grandparents is a little over seventy. These people were just moving into their teens when the Depression hit the American economy. That was the big one, where men and women were standing in bread lines and fortunes were wiped out overnight. People from that era learned how to make something out of very little; how to live a tolerable life with what they had. This may be the reason why they can relate to the kids who are down and out, physically, socially, or mentally.

Surrogate Means "Substitute"

By spotlighting the Foster Grandparent Program I believe we can emulate some of the principles that have made it so successful and add the dimension for eternal value. (Social programs have not been programmed to be Christ centered.)

In my son Tom's life, there was a surrogate grandmother who ministered to him when I was so busy in my show-business career. For many years I was more like his sister than his mother; he called my own mother Mom. His name for me was Sassie, when he was so small he couldn't pronounce Frances. His surrogate grandma was Miss Hattie, a beautiful Christian woman who took the time to talk with him, to encourage him in his faith, and to applaud his musical talent. The Lord had His hand on Tom to give him Miss Hattie when he needed her.

Nancy Reagan's parents were divorced right after she was born, and her mother went back to work to earn a living as a stage actress. When her mother was touring, Nancy lived with her aunt and uncle, who were like foster grandparents to her.

What more valuable and loving service can anyone perform than to bring love into the life of a child? Who knows how many children each foster or substitute grandparent influences for the better?

Just look around. At church there is a young woman, divorced with two small children. Her parents are a thousand miles away, and the paternal grandparents are dead. Do you have a little time to take them out for ice cream or to the park? What about the kids next door? Would they like to come and hear Bible stories or see the pictures of your last trip? Ask them over. As far as grandparents are concerned, I think there can be a substitute for the real thing.

Hit the Myths

I am tired of stereotypes of the elderly. We are not all senile, infirm, or stupid. Recently one of the major airlines had a radio commercial about a child calling his grandma and saying, "Grandma, I'm coming to visit you." After an exchange of information on the time and the flights, the conversation was ended, and then Grandma said to Grandpa, "Now who was that Nancy who called?" The image of a forgetful old woman was imprinted upon our minds.

However, there are new and encouraging trends that show that those of us over sixty are changing the public's impression of aging. Watch the aisles in the supermarkets and see how many carts containing the little basket sitters are being pushed by Grandma or Grandpa.

It's not the years, but our attitude toward aging and our physical health that determine the quality of our later years.

The finest way to preserve a quality of life after the so-called retirement age is to serve others.

When we give of ourselves, we gain. When we offer our love, we are loved. The Bible says, "Most important of all, continue to show deep love for each other, for love makes up for many of your faults. Cheerfully share your home with those who need a meal or a place to stay for the night" (1 Peter 4:8, 9).

A Place to Stay

Dusty (Roy, Jr.) and I have recorded some radio and television spots for San Bernardino County, asking for foster homes, on a short-term basis, for displaced, confused youngsters. These children would come by court referral and need understanding, love, and discipline in order to face with confidence the turbulent society in which we live.

Here is an opportunity for real grandparenting by men and women who will encourage and love these unfortunate children. Jesus said if we would lose our lives for His sake, we would find them in Him. He said to do unto others as you would have them do unto you. If we will give of ourselves to the younger generation, let them know we believe in them, that we really care, we will find our lives satisfying and full of purpose.

Grandparenting extends beyond bloodlines. One of the most important issues of our day is the way the older generation can help the younger and vice versa. We can be in the forefront of a return to the biblical values of respect for the elderly and care for the young, which Jesus taught.

Dr. Margaret Mead, an anthropologist and humanitarian, said in an interview with *Family Circle* magazine: "We in America have very little sense of interdependence. The real issue is whether a society keeps its older people close to children and young people. If old people are separated from family life, there is real tragedy both for them and for the young."

When asked by an interviewer if she thought love could heal the whole world, First Lady Nancy Reagan answered, "It certainly can do an awful lot for our society. And we certainly need more expression of it—more between parents and children, more between friend and friend, more between strangers."

Jesus said, ". . . Love each other just as much as I love you. Your strong love for each other will prove to the world that you are my disciples" (John 13:34, 35).

Surrogate grandparents have learned how to think in four-letter words:

Give

Love

Care

Live

10

... Provide a Sense of Roots

"A mule always boasts that its ancestors were horses."
A GERMAN PROVERB

I don't believe in living in the past, but the past lives in us. Grandparents, we are living history, the results of the richness of a heritage that we can will to our children and grandchildren.

We should be indebted to Alex Haley and his fascinating book, *Roots*, and to the television program that kept so many of us absorbed in the story of his ancestry. However, Haley did not invent the concept of tracing genealogy. He revived our desire to discover our origins. Libraries suddenly were deluged with requests for old newspapers and history books. People who had little interest in their family trees began to research and ask Grandma and Grandpa questions.

Many Christians who engage in a through-the-Bible personal study joyfully skip over the long chapters of "begats," but spend months unearthing the name of a great-great-great-grandfather. The Old Testament is a study in genealogy, but modern day Americans have become rootless, until recently. In our search for solidity in a shifting, uncertain world, we like to learn about times that seemed safer, more secure.

Children want to know about their parents and grandparents: What did they do when they were young, where did they live; how did they think? Okay, grandparents, now we have our chance. We can make a unique contribution by providing the biographical anecdotes that give color and reality to past generations.

King Solomon had plenty of bucks to leave to his family, yet he wrote this advice: "When a good man dies, he leaves an inheritance to his grandchildren . . ." (Proverbs 13:22). Solomon wasn't talking about an inheritance of money, but that of memories, knowledge, and history.

Biographies are written about the rich, the famous, or the infamous, and many grandparents might say, "How can I be living history? I'm not important. I've just had a very ordinary life."

No life is ordinary. God has given us experiences that no one else has had. What was mundane for us may be magic to our grandchildren.

Penny, a young woman with two small children of her own, was visiting her mother and going through some of the memorabilia her recently deceased grandmother had left. In a soiled shoe box she found some tiny handmade baby dresses, yellowed and crumpled with age. "Look at these, Mom," she said, holding up a tiny dress, "can you imagine ironing all of these every day?" One little dress had tiny, hand-crocheted flowers all over the collar and around the hem. Mother and daughter began to muse over the time it took Grandma to sew such a garment. Here was the granddaughter, discovering a treasure that only she could appreciate and taking the fragile little dress home to wash and frame for her own daughter. Did Great-grandmother know that she would be living history when she strained her eyes to put those infinitesimal stitches in a child's garment?

Our lives, grandparents, may seem ordinary to us, but they will be unusual to our grandchildren. Did you ever ride on a train across the United States, eat in a dining car while the prairies of Kansas or the mountains of Colorado whizzed by your window? Your grandchildren may never have been on a train.

Did you play kick the can or home free during long summer evenings, falling into bed exhausted, while your mother put lotion on your mosquito bites? Your grandchildren may be wondering what you did before television. They have never known what life was like before the tube.

Do you remember the corner drugstore, where the benevolent owner allowed you to sit every afternoon after school and sip five-cent cherry Cokes and flirt for two hours? Your grandchildren may have lessons, clubs, and Scouts and wonder if your life was dull without all these activities.

In the past few decades technology has advanced so fast that our grandchildren may think that transcontinental jets, instant replay of football games, and McDonald hamburgers have been permanent American fixtures. Do you think, grandparents, we have led ordinary lives? We can remember when the corner grocery store had bins of cookies and the owner would let us dip our hands in and take one or two. We remember our first airplane ride, Pearl Harbor, and V-E Day. We remember Hitler's voice on the radio and Mussolini standing on his balcony. We remember our reaction when we heard that John F. Kennedy was shot. That is living history.

No Moral to This Story

Many parents have not shared a lot about their childhood with their own children. Or perhaps they have told the same story over and over again, adding the moral in such a syrupy way that the kids are automatically turned off. However, when the grandchildren come along, it's easier just to tell the stories without moralizing. Grandchildren need to know about the dismal times, as well as the happy times. The greatest myth of all is that childhood is happy. Many times it is miserable, and knowing that others have faced hard problems will be helpful to our grandchildren when life confronts them with challenges.

One young man, growing up in a Los Angeles suburb, listened for an hour while his grandmother told him about her life in a small town. Her father had been a railroad switchman, and they lived in a two-story house near the tracks. They took in boarders for extra money, and Grandma told about the dinners around the big table, with chairs for twenty, and the mounds of potatoes and pot roast that would be consumed. After dinner everyone went into the parlor, and Grandmother played the piano and led singing. This was another time, another era, but living history for the young man who thought all music came from a stereo and the only decent potatoes were french fries smothered with catsup.

The mini-history lesson began because Grandma showed him a picture of herself sitting on a piano bench, with her very fat Dalmatian perched beside her. No moral to the story, but another thread to tie together the fragmented generations.

We are very important, grandparents, as the family historians.

Not Toynbee, Just Me

Where to start? First, with the inevitable photo albums. They may be more cumbersome, but slide projectors have a tendency to break, and movie projectors may not always be available. Pictures are always accessible.

One grandmother collected Bibles and the genealogy of the family, as well as the chronology of births, weddings, and deaths that provided a vital link in her family's history.

Consider writing your autobiography on cassette tape, or put it down in a diary. The person who knows the most about you is yourself, and someday that information only you know will be valuable to your family.

If the idea of sitting down and writing is awesome to you, try making an outline and dictating into a cassette recorder. Your grandchildren will cherish *The Chronicles of Grandma*, or whatever you wish to title it, and you will leave a legacy that can't be matched.

Talk about:

The names of your mother and father, grandmother and grandfather, and others as far back as you have traced. Tell something about them: their occupation, what happened of significance in their lives.

Where you were born, what your childhood was like.

Places you have visited.

Historic events you have witnessed.

Jobs you have had, places you have worked.

Schools you have attended.

What your parents did when you were a child.

Funny, exciting, tragic, happy things that have happened.

I realize that everyone can't build a museum, like Roy and I have in Victorville, but every grandparent can have a perpetuating family museum of the collectibles handed down from generation to generation.

What are roots, anyhow? They are the means by which the plant grows, the flower blossoms, the tree flourishes. We can let our grandchildren know our roots in Jesus Christ. How did we come to know Him? Tell them about the churches we attended, the Sunday-school teachers we remember. What a legacy!

And I pray that Christ will be more and more at home in your hearts, living within you as you trust in him. May your roots go down deep into the soil of God's marvelous love; and may you be able to feel and understand, as all

God's children should, how long, how wide, how deep, and how high his love really is; and to experience this love for yourselves, though it is so great that you will never see the end of it or fully know or understand it. And so at last you will be filled up with God himself.

Ephesians 3:17–19

11

... Lead the Way to Jesus

"I know how much you trust the Lord, just as your mother Eunice and your grandmother Lois do...."

2 Timothy 1:5

Lois was a grandmother of distinction. She lived in a little town called Lystra, which was located in what is called Turkey today. Lois and her daughter, Eunice, were Jewesses who must have attended the synagogue in a town twenty-five miles from their home. Can you imagine the difficulty these two women must have had, traveling such a long distance by foot or by donkey, to worship?

One day a couple of unusual characters came to Lois's hometown and began to work miracles. Lois probably went to the local Laundromat, where the women pounded their clothes with stones, and heard the gossip. "Did you hear about old man Ben? You know, the one who crawls through the streets on his hands and knees? Well, you'll never believe it. This fellow by the name of Paul called to him and said, 'Stand up!' and just like that Ben leaped to his feet and started to walk!"

"A miracle worker! Imagine. Paul can't be a mortal man, he must be a god."

Lois may have gathered up her laundry and run to the town square to see this man. Along the way she stopped by her daughter's house and called, "Eunice, come on out. Bring Timothy along. Some miracle workers are in town, and the people are saying they are gods in human bodies!"

The two women, holding on to little Timothy's hands, followed the crowds to the outskirts of the city. People were pushing cartloads of flowers, and some were leading their oxen along the dusty road to offer as a sacrifice to these strange "gods."

As they pushed their way through the curious onlookers, they saw two men, who were called Barnabas and Paul, shouting to the people, "Men! What are you doing? We're merely human beings like yourselves! We've come to bring you the Good News that you are invited to turn from the worship of these foolish things and to pray instead to the living God who made heaven and earth and sea and everything in them."

Lois and Eunice must have looked at each other and said, "Who are they? They are Jews, but they don't speak like our rabbis."

Perhaps the women stayed and listened to what Paul had to say. They had studied the Old Testament Scriptures and had prayed for the coming of the Messiah.

A few days later, some Jews came into Lystra from Antioch and stirred the recently admiring crowd into a murderous mob. Instead of a shower of flowers, Paul was pelted with stones and dragged to the outskirts of the city, apparently dead. The Bible tells us (Acts 14:20) that those who believed his message about Jesus Christ stood around him, and suddenly he stood up and walked back into town.

I have no way of knowing, but I can't help thinking that Lois and her daughter were among those believers who watched the miraculous recovery of Paul.

Lois, a godly grandmother, and Eunice, a faithful mother, were the teachers and examples for young Timothy, who later became like a son to the Apostle Paul.

Did Timothy's grandmother lead him to Jesus? Probably not. However, her example, her teachings, and her faith were strong influences in his life. In one of Paul's letters to Timothy, he said: "You know how, when you were a small child, you were taught the holy Scriptures; and it is these that make you wise to accept God's salvation by trusting in Christ Jesus" (2 Timothy 3:15).

Seed Planters

What can a godly grandparent do? We may plant the seeds that lead our grandchildren to seek and find Jesus Christ. It's not the preaching they hear, but the living we do that makes a difference in those precious young lives. Influence is never neutral. We're sowing seeds that will bear either a good or evil harvest.

One of the greatest women I have ever known told about a dream she had about her great-grandfather. They were walking together in a beautiful park, looking at the flowers growing in profusion along the path. He took his great-granddaughter by the hand and said, "When you sow some seed and put it in the ground, this seed will make a plant, and this plant will give seed again." He led her into the house and they sat down at the kitchen table, where he opened his well-worn Bible. "Girl, I will show you something that will never change. It is the Word of God. Plant the seeds from God's Book, and they will grow from generation to generation."

That girl was Corrie ten Boom, and the godly influence from her great-grandfather down through the generations resulted in the life of a woman who has led many spiritual children and grandchildren to know the Lord.

An energetic, mischievous young boy, Billy Frank, knew the stories about the heroism of his grandfather, a Civil War veteran. Grandfather was a one-legged, one-eyed Confederate who worked harder than most men who had two legs and eyes. When he returned from the war and began raising a family, he made daily Bible reading and prayers a regular part of the family routine. His grandson, Billy Frank, benefited from the example of Grandfather Ben Coffey, when his own mother and father emulated that godly pattern.

Billy Frank is my friend, who was lead to Jesus by a fiery Southern evangelist, Mordecai Ham. But the example of his grandparents pointed him in the right direction. Billy Frank is better known as Billy Graham.

At a bridal shower for Julie, one of Tom's daughters, an elderly friend from Emmanuel Baptist Church in Pasadena, where Tom ministered in music, said to me, "You have done a wonderful job with Tom."

I shook my head, "No, my mother did a wonderful job with him."

She looked at me, realizing that it wasn't modesty, but honesty that prompted my reply. "Come to think of it," she mused, "I heard him say the credit goes to his grandmother."

Grandparents, it's our lives they watch, not always our words they hear.

An Unbelieving Generation

Sometimes God's chain from "generation to generation" is broken. Grandparents may have unbelieving children who are the parents of unbelieving children. How can grandparents lead the children to Jesus if the barriers are erected by their parents? The answer is not easy, but it is simple: by the lives we live and the prayers we offer.

Let me tell you the story of Mary Ellen. She was raised in a home where humanism, not God, was honored. As she grew up, she was dearly loved, but never heard stories from the Bible or about Jesus Christ. Her grandmother lived hundreds of miles away, and she saw her seldom, but each time Mary Ellen was with her, grandmother told her about the love of God.

When Mary Ellen was twenty-four years old she heard the Gospel for the first time and responded wholeheartedly to accepting Jesus Christ as her Savior. Did Grandmother lead her to Jesus? Not directly. However, many years later Mary Ellen found her baby book and for the first time realized the power of the Scripture that says, ". . .The earnest prayer of a righteous man has great power and wonderful results" (James 5:16).

Grandma's letters, glued into that treasured baby book, were dated a few days after Mary Ellen's birth. This little Scottish grandmother wrote:

To my own cherub, My Wee Lamb Mary Ellen.

Grandma will say a prayer *especially for you* every day of her life. God is very good, my Wee Lambie, and if we remember Him, He never forsakes us; and I *know* that you are going to learn to love Him when you grow a little bit bigger.

God bless you,
GRANNY

Yes, He Answers Prayers

Grandparents can. . . :
Testify that God answers prayers. We've had more experience in life's rocky places and can tell the stories to our grandchildren about the way we have heard God say to us, "Yes," "No," or "Wait a while."

When my children and grandchildren go through the "valley of shadow," I want them to know that the Lord is with them, strengthening them. Prayers are answered in His way.

When our darling little Debbie was killed in a church-bus accident, another chapter of heartache was written in our lives. Before the car arrived to take us to Forest Lawn for the service, I knelt at our family altar and asked God to give me strength that I might be a good Christian witness at the service. I knew this tragedy had been spread across the newspapers of the country, and with all my heart I wanted the world to know that He holds me up when I have no power myself.

One week after the funeral I received a letter that said,

Dear Dale:

When I heard about the bus accident it was bad enough. When I heard that the daughter of Dale and Roy Rogers was in it, I wondered if your strength would hold. You had been through so much. I saw you on television at the funeral, and I think your face told the story. It was terrible agony for you, but there was a peace on your face that is seldom seen these days.

Yes, grandchildren, God does answer prayers. And grandparents, we may be the books our grandchildren read when the world tells them to follow the siren song of secularism. We may be the light they need to guide them out of the darkness of unbelief and skepticism.

Recently I've been having a lot of trouble with my eyes. Driving at night has become a little more difficult, and my arms have become too short to read a book easily. When I meet my friends who are wearing those three-paned spectacles, I'm reminded of this poem:

> Grandmother's glasses had two windows;
> And I, a child at her aproned knee,
> Would prod, "Grandmother, when you look
> Through the bottoms, what do you see?"

And she would always smile and say
That she saw only me.
And "Grandmother, when you look
Through the tops, tell, what do you see?"

"The lane, the hill, the field of hay,
The collie dog, the maple tree . . ."
When grandmother looked above her specs,
Then I would never prod.
For Grandmother's eyes grew misty blue;
I knew that she saw God.

BEULAH FENDERSON SMITH

12

. . . Pray Without Ceasing

"My Grandpa's a lot like God . . . only he doesn't have a beard."

BOBBY
Age 5

The best way to raise a child is on our knees. We should use common sense, experience, and counsel of child experts, roll them all together, and bathe them with God's strength. I've often wondered, "How does anyone live in the world today without knowing Jesus?"

I can remember how it was to live without God and know how it has been to live for Him. My life has not been easy, but I wouldn't change a thing, because I know it has been designed by the Master of the universe. He doesn't make mistakes.

He wants to hear from us. If we never communicate with Him, how will He know what we are thinking? How will He hear our appreciation for what He has done, if we don't tell Him?

My family is so large and spread out that I'm not able to communicate with them as much as I would like. For the past few years I have been on the road more that I am home. When I am home, Roy and I like to spend quiet times together, playing dominos, walking, watching favorite programs, and attending church. We can and do communicate with our heavenly Father, asking Him for specific requests for the children, grandchildren, and great-grandchildren. He's never too busy to listen.

Mindy, our first grandchild, was born with only one hip socket; I prayed hard that she would be all right. (Why do we pray when things go wrong and forget, so often, to thank the Lord when we're getting along fine?) Let me share the story of answers to prayers in the life of grown-up Mindy, her husband, Jon Petersen, and their three small children.

Mindy was not raised in deprivation, nor in the lap of luxury. Her parents, Tom and Barbara, were not what you would call affluent, since they minister with music in churches, and Tom taught public-school music in a junior high for several years before that. However, they gave their children every advantage that was possible and have been marvelous Christian parents.

Mindy always wanted to be a missionary, and Jon was raised in a mission-school environment. They gave up a brand new home in Grants Pass, Oregon, to be available to minister wherever the Lord called them. They trained for mission work with Youth With a Mission, on the Kona coast of Hawaii, and are now stationed in Amsterdam, Holland. That may sound like glamor, but listen to this:

Well, we are finally settled in our community life-style here on Kona, and we really love it! There's such rest in being in the "bull's-eye" of God's will. The village here is very international. This is really a launching pad for many missionaries into the Asia and Pacific regions. Just in the past three days, for instance, we had people arrive from Australia, Holland, Thailand, and Saipan. And we sent out a family to refugee camps in Somalia—and our director, to a leadership conference of 800 nationals in Korea, where he commissioned thirty new national pastors! So you can understand the world exposure we're getting here. Our eyes and hearts are being opened up to the tremendous needs of the lost and the Lord's church in other parts of the world—and in Third World countries in particular. We feel no loss at having left a "secure" comfortable life, only tremendous privilege to have been called. *God has mighty things to accomplish through His people in these last days* [italics mine].

Part of our burden, too, is to be used to help the American church to see things in a more realistic view. Statistically, there is not a food shortage on the planet. The food is simply not balanced in its distribution. We Americans could cut back on so much and still live like kings comparatively. I am now eating to survive and be healthy, and not just because I like to eat.

She went on to give me sample meals, healthy food, well balanced for their physical well-being. She said her husband and children were thriving beautifully. As for herself, she wrote:

And me, well you can probably tell from the tone of this letter that I'm thrilled to be here. We've gone through some difficult adjustments, but each time we find that God has built into us more trust than the time before and has made us more flexible. So the big thing with me is a time of setting priorities straight and learning to grow.

The beautiful part of their training for nine months is the fact that their family is together in this venture. There are no cars, no luxuries; they are enjoying each other in a rather stringent regimen and finding real life in Christ, not in things. She said she has learned to just look in stores and not buy.

My mission field is not the same as Mindy's, but I can pray for her and the family as they reach out to people I might not be able to touch.

Do you sense an awareness of the need to return to good

family relationships, instead of overemphasis on material acquisitions? It's a most healthy sign, so let's keep on praying!

Security Blanket

Watching television recently, I listened with fascination to Dr. Linder explain the effects of the drug PCP, often known as "angel dust." The good doctor called it "devil dust," which is more appropriate. There were some shocking film clips of PCP victims. He explained that the only way to overcome the temptation to experience the PCP "high" (a false feeling of power, security, fast-mind acrobatics) was the security of a loving family, belief in God, and prayer. He admitted that medical science had no real cure.

Ben Kinchlow, the cohost on the 700 Club, was acquainted with drugs during the B.C. times (before Christ in his life) and said there was no such thing as "cold turkey" quitting—that Jesus Christ was the true liberator from drugs. Amen and amen!

Jesus is the true liberator of all that harms us in body, mind, and spirit. This has been my own experience, although I have never indulged in mind-bending drugs.

When Dr. Linder stressed the family as a security blanket, he mentioned that a survey showed many fathers spent about forty seconds per day with their children. Grandpa, where are you? You most certainly are a father image to that grandchild. Fill the gap!

Telephone Lines Are Never Down

The phone companies have some touching advertisements of grandchildren calling grandparents and vice versa. Faces light up and bills go up as the ad campaign is effective. God's lines are never busy, and the circuits are in good repair. It's not always possible or feasible for us to touch or talk to each other, but we can always pray.

Here is what Billy Graham's dear mother wrote in her book *They Call Me Mother Graham*:

> Since the children have married and gone their separate ways, and since my husband's death, I have found myself with more time to devote to prayer. I pray without ceasing for Billy and the tremendous responsibility that God has given to him; but also for my other children, my thirteen grandchildren, fourteen great-grandchildren (at the time of this writing), and for world wide needs.
>
> I often wonder if we, as mothers, recognize how much our prayers have influenced our children's choices through life. It is something we should contemplate seriously.

I spend so much time on airplanes and find those isolated moments in the sky are wonderful times to write a few thoughts and to pray. People won't bother you when you have your eyes closed, but God can be your seat companion, listening and caring.

When I have speaking and singing engagements, there is no time for socializing before or after an appearance. My little hotel room is an oasis from the world where I can hole up and pray out loud without interruptions.

Take a moment to place a long-distance message on someone's behalf. You may be calling at just the right time!

We Love 'Em so Much It Hurts

How can we explain it unless we've experienced it? There's something so special about being a grandparent, and sometimes we feel so helpless in the role.

We do have an important part in their battles with the pressures of life, providing stability in a changing world; but we must be careful to let them know that true security is in a personal relationship to God, through our Lord Jesus Christ. The song "They Will Know We Are Christians by Our Love" could be our theme. Grandchildren are no dummies; they will know if we really believe in Jesus. I am amazed how they can cut straight through the facade of a phoney.

Grandparents without Jesus can build memories, be fun, listen to their problems, provide a sense of roots and tradition— all those good things—but the most important quality we can give them will be missing.

I'm not making any sanctimonious statements without a backup. I have no righteousness of my own, but I have claimed the righteousness of Jesus Christ and claim His righteousness as my own. The Bible says: "...The earnest prayer of a righteous man has great power and wonderful results" (James 5:16).

When I pray, I expect God's power to work. I have claimed that verse for my children and grandchildren, just as my mother claimed it for me through those twenty-five years of wandering from the teachings she gave me.

We can love and pray and live our faith in front of our children and grandchildren and trust God for the rest. We cannot live their lives for them; they are accountable to God, but we can live a consistent life before them. They must see something in us to command respect.

Final Rules for Grandparents

1. Accept your age.

It's wonderful to have the years behind us, the experience of living. Face-lifts and crash diets will not make us teenagers again. The miles are recorded inside us. We know where we have been and how long we've been on the road.

The Bible gives us a guide to clothing: "Therefore, as God's chosen people, holy and dearly loved, clothe yourselves with compassion, kindness, humility, gentleness and patience" (Colossians 3:12 NIV).

However, let's not get sloppy in our personal appearance. It's not vanity for Grandmother to have her hair done or for Grandpa to wear snappy clothes; it's sanity.

2. Don't hold grudges.

A grandparent who doesn't accept his daughter-in-law or son-in-law or who criticizes them to the rest of the family can't expect to earn the respect of his grandchildren.

In that wonderful passage in Colossians that spells out the "rules for holy living," it says: "Bear with each other and forgive what ever grievances you may have against one another. Forgive as the Lord forgave you" (Colossians 3:13 NIV).

I have known grandparents who vent their displeasure with their own children or in-laws through the grandchildren. They say such things as, "Don't your parents ever check what you're wearing before you go out?" Or, "Why is your hair so dirty; doesn't your mother wash it?"

A grudge will make a grump out of Gram and Gramps.

3. Stay young in heart.

The same story repeated over and over is one of the best ways to turn off young ears. You could say, "Have I told you about . . .?" And if you have, forget it. Vain repetitions are a sure way to canceled communications.

4. Learn and teach Bible principles.

If the world is pushing our grandchildren into its mold, show them what the Word of God has to say about the major temptations they face. The Bible says; "Let the word of Christ dwell in you richly as you teach and admonish one another with all

wisdom and as you sing psalms, hymns and spiritual songs
with gratitude in your hearts to God" (Colossians 3:16 NIV).

5. *Keep your sense of humor.*

A friend was telling me about taking her three-year-old
granddaughter shopping. Grandma lost her briefly in a clothing store, and after a few frantic moments of calling her name,
she saw the little culprit, stark naked, standing on a raised
platform beside a mannequin. The astonished grandmother
grabbed the little nudist just as she shouted, "Grandma, I have
to go to the bathroom." Only a keen sense of humor will suffice in a ridiculous situation.

We need to laugh at ourselves. We have enough miles recorded in us to know the therapy of hilarity.

6. *Pray continually.*

Frequently we may think, "I've tried everything else, now I
might as well pray." Today I pray first and fly later. The Lord
tells us to pray for everything, and that means the little, insig-
nificant things as well as major issues. Pray for His angels to
surround the grandchildren and keep them free from harm.
Pray for them to accept Him and love Him. Pray for wisdom
for the parents and understanding during the times when
things look bleak. Pray with thanksgiving.

Trouble may drive us to prayer, but prayer will drive trouble
away.

How Important Are We?

I saw two license plates on cars parked side by side in a car-
port. One said, "GAM 77," and the other said, "GAMP 77."
That couple was so delighted with their new status as grandparents in the year 1977 that they displayed it publicly.

Across the street was another car with a license that said,
"Happiness is being a grandparent."

After the blush of pride is over, what can we do?

Grandparents can make a unique contribution. We can love when they are the most unlovable, because we remember what their parents did. We can play when Mom and Dad are too busy or too tired, because we slowed down and have more time. We can listen when no one else seems to care, because we've heard almost everything in our lifetimes.

We can heal wounds with the balm of experience. We can provide bridges across troubled waters when parents and kids are churning. We can be available when the world doesn't seem to care.

We have been called by God to do things no one else can do. How privileged we are to be such chosen people. Come on, grandparents, join us in prayer to change the world we touch with the magic of love.

"May the Lord continually bless you with heaven's blessing as well as with human joys. May you live to enjoy your grandchildren! . . ." (Psalms 128:5, 6).

Appendix: Books and Records for Grandchildren

Gift Books for Grandchildren

What to buy? Goodness, I have such trouble picking out books when there are so many good ones in the stores today. There is a wealth of good reading available for all ages, from toddlers to teenagers. Old classics and new releases line the shelves and invite us to consider their merits. It's puzzling to know just which book to choose for each child.

The following book-buying guidelines have helped me discover books that match each grandchild's age, interests, and needs.

Georgiana Walker, who compiled these lists, has helped me with suggested titles of longtime favorites, as well as new titles. There are many creative approaches to communicating Christian values and biblical principles. Just looking at the marvelous illustrations make many of the books a visual treat.

How gratifying it is, grandparents, to give young people quality books, full of beauty, truth, and hours of enjoyment.

Books for the Very Young
(Ages Six Months to Two Years)

Cardboard books, with their sturdy pages, are excellent for babies and young toddlers. Plastic and cloth books also provide much enjoyment without the frustration of torn pages.

Baby's First Book; Baby's First Toys; Baby Animals. New York: Platt & Munk. Teddy-Board Books. Spiral-bound cardboard books that open flat. Excellent first books.

God Made Food; God Made Animals. Ventura, Calif.: Regal Books, 1981. Nontoxic, washable cloth books with realistic, bright pictures to talk about and identify.

Green Frog; Friends. St. Louis: Concordia, 1975. Caterpillar Books series. Clear, colorful pictures, brief text. Good to talk about books with details in pictures for child to discover.

I Can Do It by Myself. New York: Golden Press, 1981. Illustrated by June Golsborough. Delightful pictures of at-home scenes. Excellent for pointing to and talking about and discovering what a child can do.

Just Before Bed Time; God Made Me. Norwalk, Conn.: C. R. Gibson. Plastic books of songs, rhymes, and prayers. Appealing illustrations. *God Made Me* encourages awareness: "God made my eyes . . . God made my ears . . . my hair . . . my feet . . . God made all of me."

Kundhart, Dorothy. *Pat the Bunny.* New York: Golden Press, 1962. A longtime favorite. Heavy paper pages. Each page provides a texture to feel or something to do.

McNaught, Harry. *Baby Animals.* New York: Random House, 1976. Animals are large and clearly drawn. Good for learning animal names and introducing sounds animals make.

Murphy, Elspeth. *Jesus Is God's Son; Jesus Does Good Things; Jesus Tells About God.* Elgin, Ill.: David C. Cook, 1981. Small, easy-to-hold board books. Bright pictures and simple text.

Pfloog, Jan. *Animals on the Farm.* New York: Golden Press, 1977. Fine realistic illustrations. Good for conversation: "God made the strong horse. God made the friendly cow."

Scarry, Richard. *What Animals Do.* New York: Golden Press, 1968. A thin, tall book with much to talk about. One sentence on each page tells what each animal does: "The kangaroo hops."

Books for Preschoolers
(Ages Two to Five)

God's Beautiful World; Jesus Make Me Happy; God Made Kittens. Cincinnati: Standard Publishing, 1980. Happy Day Books include twenty-one additional titles. Inexpensive, well-done books, reminiscent in size and format of the familiar Little Golden Books. Look at these—delightful!

Hymns; Prayers for Children; My Little Golden Book About God. New York: Golden Press. These are a few of the religious titles available in the Little Golden Book format. Fine illustrations, songs, poems, prayers, and simple text make these inexpensive books real treasures to share with young grandchildren.

Coriell, Ron and Rebekah. *A Child's Book of Character Building; A Child's Book of Character Building, Book 2.* Old Tappan, N.J.: Fleming H. Revell, 1980. Read-to-me stories that teach children good character traits. Each trait has a story about children at school, at home, at play, and a Bible story with Scripture references. A great teaching tool for parents.

Decker, Marjorie. *The Christian Mother Goose Book; The Christian Mother Goose Treasury.* Old Tappan, N.J.: Fleming H. Revell, 1980. Children enjoy the rhyming language and lively jingles of these rewritten Mother Goose rhymes, paraphrased to communicate Christian concepts. Colorfully illustrated.

Dienert, Ruth Graham. *First Steps in the Bible.* Waco, Tex.: Word Books, 1982. Simple language tells basic Bible stories and relates biblical truth to child's experience. A quality book: heavy paper, beautiful format, appealing photographs.

Field, Rachel. *Prayer for a Child.* New York: Collier Books, 1973. Beautifully illustrated prayer that gently relates child's life to God's love and care. Randolph Caldecott Medal winner—a classic.

Lindvall, Ella K. *Read-Aloud Bible Stories, Volume 1.* Evanston, Ill.: Moody Press, 1982. Five favorite stories about Jesus, with bold, bright illustrations and action-filled text. Written especially for preschoolers and early–school-age children. A special book. Large, two-lap size.

Lobel, Arnold. *Frog and Toad Together; Frog and Toad Are Friends; Frog and Toad All Year.* New York: Harper & Row. Frog and Toad are great friends for children and the adults who share the stories. These books acquaint children with the seasons, the value of caring about one another, and much more.

Milne, A. A. *Winnie the Pooh; The House at Pooh Corner.* New York: Dutton. Winnie the Pooh and his friends Piglet, Eeyore, Rabbit, Kanga, and Baby Roo have been favorites of young children (and older children, too) since the 1920s. Pooh stories are available in many formats.

Murphy, Elspeth. *What Can I Say to God? Sometimes I Get Lonely; Where Are You, God?* Elgin, Ill.: Chariot Books. Verses from the Psalms, paraphrased in the language of young children, help the child learn of God's greatness and presence at all times. (There are seven books in the David and I Talk to God series.)

Wilt, Joy. *You're All Right; Mine and Yours; You're One of a Kind.* Waco, Tex.: Word Books. The Joy Wilt series. A step-by-step series to help a child understand himself and relationships. There are twenty-four books in this series.

Books for School-Age Children
Early School Age (Six Through Eight)

As the child's experiences multiply and interests expand so do the possibilities for books that will please the youngster. Here are just a few of the fine books that widen understanding and bring joy.

David; Daniel; Josuah; Noah; Paul. Elgin, Ill.: Chariot Books. These titles, along with others, make up the Burl Ives Bible Stories With Tapes. Each story pack includes a colorful book and cassette tape of the story, told by Burl Ives.

Exploring Kittens. San Francisco: Heian International, 1980. Photos by Nobuo Honda. Eighty-eight pages of fascinating color photos of kittens. Text is less than two pages, to introduce photographs. Youngsters will thoroughly enjoy the kittens—so will the entire family.

Jonah. Westchester, Ill.: Cornerstone Books, 1981. Illustrated by Kurt Mitchell. Text from the New International Version of the Bible, foreword by Edith Schaeffer. After you discover this book, it may be difficult to give it away—even to a grandchild. Jonah is pictured as a mouse being sent by God into a city of sleek cats. Truly good art. A large book, a future classic.

The Thief Who Was Sorry; Nicodemus Learns the Way; The Lord's Prayer. St. Louis: Concordia. Arch Books are an ongoing series of freshly rhymed, attractively illustrated Bible stories. Also available as Arch Books Aloud. Each Aloud set includes two Arch Books and the stories told on one tape cassette.

Hall, Donald. *Ox-Cart Man.* New York: Viking Press, 1980. Engaging full-color illustrations create the mood of another time and place: nineteenth-century New England. The theme is the work the family does together to grow the crops and care for their animals. A Randolph Caldecott Medal winner.

Kashuya, Masahiro. *The Beginning of the World.* Nashville: Abingdon, 1982. The story of God creating all things, told in beautiful, cheerful paintings. Helps acquaint the child with God the Creator, reverently, with few words.

Moore, Judy Hull. *God's Plan for the Seashore; God's Plan for Seasons; God's Plan for Birds.* Evanston, Ill.: Moody Press, 1980. God in Creation series. Colorfully illustrated with a blend of artwork and photographs. Easy-to-read text, pictures

to color, follow-the-dot fun. Books to enjoy. Books that teach.
Nystrom, Carolyn. *Who Is Jesus? Who Is God? What Is Prayer? The Holy Spirit in Me.* Evanston, Ill.: Moody Press, 1980. Questions children wonder about and ask are skillfully answered in direct, simple language. Colorful contemporary art illustrates the text.
Roberts, Evelyn. *Heaven Has a Floor.* New York: Dial Press, 1979. When young Jon Oral lost his parents in a plane crash, he asked, "Does heaven have a floor?" This book is his grandmother's sensitive answer. Notes with Scripture references for parents to explore provide biblical authority for the statements about heaven.
Spiers, Peter. *People.* New York: Doubleday, 1980. An oversize picture book that helps a child see people from all over the world. Color and detail are superb. Much for a child to see and learn about "Red and yellow, black and white, all are precious in His sight. . . ."
Winston Press Editorial Staff, eds. *The Christmas Pageant.* Minneapolis, Minn.: Winston Press, 1979. Illustrated by Tomie de Paola. Text from Matthew and Luke. Refreshing art retells the story of Jesus' birth as the children of the book act out the story. A center section provides puppet characters for your grandchild to create his or her own Christmas story. Find this lovely book now and save it for Christmastime.

School-Age Children
Older Children (Ages Eight Through Twelve)

Although children's reading skills vary widely, the eight-to twelve-year-old span can be exciting years of discovery for young readers. Try to choose books that match your grandchild's reading level, but do provide opportunities for him or her to explore the realities of faraway times and places, out-of-this-world fantasies, and the wonders of now.

Barrett, Ethel. *Ruth.* Ventura, Calif.: Regal Books, 1980. Well-known for her storytelling skills, Barrett retells this Old Testament tale with tenderness, beauty, and suspense. She has also written the stories of Joshua, Joseph, Daniel, and Paul for young readers. All are published by Regal.

Burnett, Frances Hodgson. *The Secret Garden.* Milwaukee, Wis.: Raintree Children's Books, 1978. A wonderful story of an unhappy, physically handicapped boy and the two children who help him make a happy discovery. Read it yourself before you give it to a grandchild.

Couldridge, Rhoda. *Christian's Journey—John Bunyan's Pilgrim's Progress.* Nashville: Abingdon, 1980. Excellent retelling of Bunyan's allegory helps child glimpse the Christian's journey through life. Delightful artwork by a child.

Gaines, M. C., ed. *Picture Stories from the Bible.* New York: Scarf Press, 1980. Stories from the Old Testament and the New Testament, illustrated in full-color comic-strip form. This is a format children respond readily to—and read. Words of Christ are printed in red.

Grahame, Kenneth. *Wind in the Willows.* New York: Holt, Rinehart & Winston, 1980. Well-known classic loved by millions. Your grandchild will like making friends with Mole, Water Rat, Badger, and Toad. Morality is not mentioned, but it permeates the actions of the animals—real people under their fur.

Hasler, Evaline. *Martin Is Our Friend.* Nashville: Abingdon, 1981. Martin is different from the other children in his apartment. His inability to think or walk as fast as they do makes it difficult for the other children to understand Martin. An experience with a horse brings all the children together. A fine book for encouraging respect for and acceptance of one another.

Keller, W. Phillip. *A Child's Look at the Twenty-Third Psalm.*

New York: Doubleday, 1981. The child's understanding of the Psalm grows as the book tells facts about sheep and shepherding.

Krasilovsky, Phyllis. *The First Tulips in Holland.* New York: Doubleday, 1982. A beautiful big book, created by a well-known children's author, illustrated by S. D. Schindler. This story of how tulips first came to Holland is a treat of pictures and words.

Lewis, C. S. *The Chronicles of Narnia: The Lion, the Witch and the Wardrobe; Prince Caspian; The Voyage of the Dawn Treader; The Silver Chair; The Horse and His Boy; The Magician's Nephew; The Last Battle.* New York: Macmillan. These Christian children's books, favorites of our century, take youngsters to enchanted lands, where they discover shining truths of Christianity woven through the fairy tales. Some children as young as seven and eight enjoy listening to the Lewis fantasies. Advanced readers explore these special books on their own—with joy.

MacDonald, George. *The Christmas Stories of George MacDonald.* Elgin, Ill.: David C. Cook, 1981. Illustrated by Linda Hill Griffith. A collection of the Christmas tales told by this beloved Scottish storyteller. This colorfully illustrated hardback will be a family favorite.

Paterson, Katherine. *The Great Gilly Hopkins.* New York: Harper & Row, 1978. The story of a lonely foster child and the difference between being tough and being strong. There's fun, humor, and tenderness in this John Newbery Medal book. About the author: a fine Christian writer of a number of award-winning children's books. Look for her *Bridge to Terebithia; Angels and Other Strangers;* and *Jacob I Have Loved,* all published by Crowell.

Richardson, Arleta. *Stories from Grandma's Attic.* Elgin, Ill.: David C. Cook, 1980. Happy nostalgia, especially for girls. A warmhearted view of family life in the late 1800s in the Midwest.

Schoolland, Miriam M. *Leading Little Ones to God.* Grand Rapids, Mich., Wm. B. Eerdmans Publishing Company. A newly illustrated edition of a fine old classic. A book for parents and child to share. Bible stories well told.

Wangerin, Walter. *The Bible: Its Story for Children.* Chicago: Rand McNally, 1981. The author of this 416-page book of well-written stories is the Lutheran minister whose award-winning *The Book of the Dun Cow* has been read and loved by many young people. A richly illustrated book, with 250 full-color pictures.

Wilder, Laura Ingalls. *Little House in the Big Woods; These Happy Golden Years.* New York: Harper & Row. First and last titles of the eight *Little House* books. Told as fiction, the stories cover the author's life from four years to eighteen and give today's boys and girls a taste of pioneer life in the late 1800s. Also provides glimpses of family life where happiness was not tied to possessions but was found in facing hardships and good times together.

Books for Teenagers

Before buying books for a teenage grandchild, you need to know who that teenager is. Teens are very much their own people, with definite interests and preferences. Find out about your grandchild's hobbies, sports interests, work experiences, career ambitions, church involvement, and his or her faith before you go book buying. Show your love by respecting the young person's likes and dislikes.

The following suggestions are based on books teenagers choose for themselves.

Fantasies

Lewis, C. S. *The Chronicles of Narnia.* New York: Macmillan. Each of Lewis's seven *Chronicles* is popular with teenagers who enjoy fantasy. Why not give one at a time, on special days, to a grandchild? Begin with *The Lion, the Witch and the Wardrobe* and follow with *Prince Caspian, The Voyage of the Dawn Treader, The Silver Chair, The Horse and His Boy, The Magician's Nephew,* and *The Last Battle.* Teenagers will discover more of Lewis's allegories and their meaning than when (and if) they read the books as children.

Siegel, Robert. *Alpha Centauri.* Westchester, Ill.: Cornerstone, 1980. Intriguing story of truth in another time and place—the world of the centaurs and their human enemies, the Rock Movers. Siegel has woven wonderful allegorical threads into this exciting narrative.

Tolkien, J. R. R. *The Hobbit; The Lord of the Rings.* Boston: Houghton Mifflin. Tolkien creates whole new worlds and peoples and takes his readers captive. Principles of Christianity shape the action, but are never obvious. The adventures are set in Middle Earth, which finally becomes free when the Dark Lord is defeated as the One Ring of power is destroyed.

Wangerin, Walter. *The Book of the Dun Cow.* New York: Harper & Row, 1978. A fantasy high in medieval atmosphere and gusty humor. Characters are a cast of imperfect animals battling for their lives and beliefs in a timeless war between good and evil.

The Christian Life

Brand, Paul, and Yancy, Philip. *Fearfully and Wonderfully Made.* Grand Rapids, Mich.: Zondervan, 1980. For older teenagers. While they will probably skip through the text, they will discover much about the wonder of who they are—man, a complex creation of God. Encouragement for a personal relationship with Him.

Hartley, Fred. *Dare to Be Different.* Old Tappan, N.J.: Fleming H. Revell, 1980. Encourages teenagers to accept their individuality, instead of following the crowd. Describe the problems of peer pressure and points out the need for Christ in the teen's life.

Hartley, Fred. *Growing Pains: First Aid for Teenagers.* Old Tappan, N.J.: Fleming H. Revell, 1981. Helps teens handle the hard times with advice on self-esteem, parents, dating, conscience, the future, and problems.

Hartley, Fred. *Update,* Old Tappan, N.J.: Fleming H. Revell, 1977. A guide to dating that helps teens deal with all the accompanying problems.

Kesler, Jay. *Growing Places,* Old Tappan, N.J.: Fleming H. Revell, 1977. Devotions based on the promises God has given His people. The light touch the author uses will encourage teens to spend time in prayer.

Klug, Ron. *Lord, I've Been Thinking.* Minneapolis, Minn.: Augsburg, 1980. Eighty-three true-to-life prayers to help teenage boys express their feelings to God. Touches on problems, relationships with self, others, and God.

Naylor, Phyllis Reynolds. *Change in the Wind.* Minneapolis, Minn.: Augsburg, 1980. Award-winning author shows how teenagers deal with feelings, problems, and questions. Points to a wide variety of ways God helps teens grapple with life's challenges. Not heavy reading.

Ridenour, Fritz. *How to Be a Christian Without Being Religious.* Ventura, Calif.: Regal Books, 1967. Basic truths and encouragement for the Christian life, from the Book of Romans, combined with quotes from *The Living Bible Paraphrase* and clever cartoons. A great book—Ridenour's books are read by millions of young people. Ask for his other titles.

Fiction

Hill, Grace Livingston. *A Daily Rate; The Girl from Montana; The Man of the Desert; The Story of a Whim; An Unwilling Guest.* Old Tappan, N.J.: Fleming H. Revell, 1982. A series of reprints of some of the author's early novels about young girls who find romance and commit their lives to Christ. Each has an unusual background and an exciting adventure.

Jenkins, Jerry B. *Margo; Karlyn; Hilary.* Evanston, Ill.: Moody Press, 1980. First three books in an ongoing mystery series. Combines fine suspense with good storytelling. Jenkins, former director of *Moody Monthly* magazine and now directing editor of Moody Press, has written numerous books that appeal to teenagers. Ask for other titles.

Johnson, James L. *Code Name Sebastian; The Last Train from Canton.* Grand Rapids, Mich.: Zondervan. Two of the Sebastian thrillers, written by the coordinator of the journalism department at Wheaton College Graduate School. These books are fine reading for older teenagers. Inquire at your bookstore for other books in this series.

Biography

Porter, Alyene. *Papa Was a Preacher.* Old Tappan, N.J.: Spire Books, 1979. Vignettes from the family life of a preacher's daughter. The high jinks of this lively group will have teens roaring with laughter.

Wilkerson, David. *The Cross and the Switchblade.* Old Tappan, N.J.: Spire Books, 1963. An exciting story of David Wilkerson's work with ghetto teens, bringing them to know Christ. The story of his amazing success will touch many hearts.

The list could go on forever. Teenagers enjoy books like biography, animal stories, books on sports, and romances, as well as fact books and nonfiction that zeroes in on their interests.

If you really want to be the supplier of good reading for your teenage grandchildren, visit bookstores often, particularly your Christian bookstore. Ask the person who handles the books for teenagers to point out something that will appeal to young people the age of your grandchild.

Happy book shopping and happy reading for all your grandkids.

Gift Records for Grandchildren

Records are especially fine gifts for the child or teenager who is interested in music. Also, the youngster who does not enjoy reading is often a great listener.

Joyful Noise, Bill Ingram, arranger, Lillenas, 1982. Twelve contagious tunes that invite children to join in the truly joyful noise. Except for "All Night, All Day" and "Fairest Lord Jesus" the selections are fresh, unfamiliar, but easy-to-learn songs.

The Kid's Praise Album, produced by Ernie and Debbie Rettino, Maranatha Music, 1980. Simple but lively arrangements are performed entirely by children. A happy record, aimed at teaching children that there's a difference between just singing songs and truly praising God.

The Very Best of the Very Best for Kids, The Bill Gaither Trio, Word Records, 1980. Twenty joyful songs sung in the wholesome, rhythmic Gaither style. Although the songs touch on a variety of aspects of the Christian life, the central theme is "You're something special! God loves you!"

Little Big Lunch, Sonny Salsbury with Fletch Wiley, arranger, Word Records, 1982. Easy-to-learn, hard-to-forget tunes with narration that retells the miracle of Christ with the loaves and the fishes. Delightful orchestration and choral work. Good listening for children.

Super Gang: On the Road for Jesus, produced by Tom and Robin Brooks, Star Song, 1981. Two albums that combine fine energetic music and dramatic interaction that help children know what it means to trust Jesus and live His way. On the inside of the double cover of *On the Road for Jesus* is a board game that makes this album special fun for elementary-age children.

Agapeland Series

You will want to look at the five following records as possible gifts for your school-age grandchildren. The Agapeland Series is produced by Candle and distributed by Sparrow Records. The records feature well-crafted lyrics, set to a wide range of music styles, performed by very talented musicians. Some of the records are developed around a story, usually well presented, the plot reinforced by the songs.

Music Machine, 1977. In Agapeland, children discover the Music Machine. It's a noisy contraption that turns almost anything into a song. Galatians 5:22 becomes nine brilliant songs, each about a fruit of the Spirit.

Bullfrogs and Butterflies, 1978. Lively, spontaneous tunes. Great for a sing-along. There is no story line, just a fine collection of fun songs that tell about life in God's kingdom. Quality and content excellent.

Nathaniel the Grublet, 1979. A tale about a kind of dwarf, Nathaniel the Grublet, his puppy, and other grublets. As a children's morality play the story comes into focus when grublets begin stealing instead of doing honest work. Story and songs provide good entertainment and a clear contrast of good and evil. A good record to talk about with children.

Sir Oliver's Song, 1979. Sir Oliver, an owl, is the MC who leads a choir of children from all over the world as they sing about the "ten royal decrees"—Ten Commandments. The music has a definite international flavor. You will hear various stylized rhythms: polka, Irish jig, folk, calypso, and other familiar forms. Some of the songs are outstanding.

The National Philharmonic Orchestra of London Plays Agapeland for the Whole Family, 1982. A fine medley of tunes from *The Music Machine, Bullfrogs and Butterflies,* and *Sir Oliver's Song.* A record that will be played over and over for its great sound.

Records for Teenagers

Never Say Die, Petra, Star Song, 1981. Recipient of a 1981 award of merit from *Campus Life, Never Say Die* features several songs that make powerful statements about commitment to Christ. Music style: Christian pop/rock.

One of the Dominoes, Mark Heard, Home Sweet Home, 1981. This record speaks to those in high school and college who are torn between love for Christ and attraction of the world. With a contemporary rock sound, Mark deals with difficult issues facing Christians today.

In Concert Volume 2, Amy Grant, Myrrh, 1981. A favorite Christian female vocalist demonstrates her fine talent in this concert, recorded live at Oral Roberts University. From delicate soft music to foot-stomping tunes, the music shows the range and versatility of this talented singer.

Joni's Song, Joni Eareckson, Word Records, 1981. Joni Eareckson is well known as a best-selling author, artist, and actress. She is also a quadriplegic—injured in a diving accident. Now in her debut album she is a convincingly good singer. The finest song of the album is "Journey's End." Will be especially appreciated by teenagers who have read Joni's books.

The Hobbit and the Fellowship of the Ring, read by J. R. R.

Tolkien, Caedmon Records, 1952, 1981. In 1952 Tolkien was discouraged because he could not find a publisher for his trilogy, *The Lord of the Rings*. At that time he recorded excerpts from his earlier book *The Hobbit*. The readings on this album are from those recordings. This record is a must for young people who have read and enjoyed Tolkien's writings. Side 1: readings from the riddle scene from chapter five of *The Hobbit*. Side 2: short excerpts from *The Lord of the Rings*.

CHRISTIAN HERALD ASSOCIATION AND ITS MINISTRIES

CHRISTIAN HERALD ASSOCIATION, founded in 1878, publishes The Christian Herald Magazine, one of the leading interdenominational religious monthlies in America. Through its wide circulation, it brings inspiring articles and the latest news of religious developments to many families. From the magazine's pages came the initiative for CHRISTIAN HERALD CHILDREN'S HOME and THE BOWERY MISSION, two individually supported not-for-profit corporations.

CHRISTIAN HERALD CHILDREN'S HOME, established in 1894, is the name for a unique and dynamic ministry to disadvantaged children, offering hope and opportunities which would not otherwise be available for reasons of poverty and neglect. The goal is to develop each child's potential and to demonstrate Christian compassion and understanding to children in need.

Mont Lawn is a permanent camp located in Bushkill, Pennsylvania. It is the focal point of a ministry which provides a healthful "vacation with a purpose" to children who without it would be confined to the streets of the city. Up to 1000 children between the ages of 7 and 11 come to Mont Lawn each year.

Christian Herald Children's Home maintains year-round contact with children by means of an *In-City Youth Ministry*. Central to its philosophy is the belief that only through sustained relationships and demonstrated concern can individual lives be truly enriched. Special emphasis is on individual guidance, spiritual and family counseling and tutoring. This follow-up ministry to inner-city children culminates for many in financial assistance toward higher education and career counseling.

THE BOWERY MISSION, located at 227 Bowery, New York City, has since 1879 been reaching out to the lost men on the Bowery, offering them what could be their last chance to rebuild their lives. Every man is fed, clothed and ministered to. Countless numbers have entered the 90-day residential rehabilitation program at the Bowery Mission. A concentrated ministry of counseling, medical care, nutrition therapy, Bible study and Gospel services awakens a man to spiritual renewal within himself.

These ministries are supported solely by the voluntary contributions of individuals and by legacies and bequests. Contributions are tax deductible. Checks should be made out either to CHRISTIAN HERALD CHILDREN'S HOME or to THE BOWERY MISSION.

Administrative Office: 40 Overlook Drive, Chappaqua, New York 10514
Telephone: (914) 769-9000